Wrestling

The Ultimate Guide for Beginners Wanting to Learn Wrestling Techniques for Self-Defense, Physical Prowess, or Competition

© Copyright 2024 – All rights reserved.

The content contained within this book may not be reproduced, duplicated, or transmitted without direct written permission from the author or the publisher.

Under no circumstances will any blame or legal responsibility be held against the publisher, or author, for any damages, reparation, or monetary loss due to the information contained within this book, either directly or indirectly.

Legal Notice:

This book is copyright protected. It is only for personal use. You cannot amend, distribute, sell, use, quote or paraphrase any part of the content within this book, without the consent of the author or publisher.

Disclaimer Notice:

Please note the information contained within this document is for educational and entertainment purposes only. All effort has been executed to present accurate, up-to-date, reliable, and complete information. No warranties of any kind are declared or implied. Readers acknowledge that the author is not engaging in the rendering of legal, financial, medical, or professional advice. The content within this book has been derived from various sources. Please consult a licensed professional before attempting any techniques outlined in this book.

By reading this document, the reader agrees that under no circumstances is the author responsible for any losses, direct or indirect, that are incurred as a result of the use of the information contained within this document, including, but not limited to, errors, omissions, or inaccuracies.

Table of Contents

INTRODUCTION 1
CHAPTER 1: WHY SHOULD I CHOOSE WRESTLING? 3
CHAPTER 2: BASIC RULES AND SKILLS 14
CHAPTER 3: POSTURE AND BALANCE 24
CHAPTER 4: PENETRATING, LIFTING, AND OTHER MANEUVERS 36
CHAPTER 5: HOW TO ATTACK AND COUNTERATTACK 49
CHAPTER 6: REVERSAL TECHNIQUES 60
CHAPTER 7: ESCAPE TECHNIQUES 69
CHAPTER 8: PINNING COMBINATIONS 78
CHAPTER 9: TRAINING AT HOME 86
CHAPTER 10: TRAINING AND COACHING YOUTH 95
CHAPTER 11: WRESTLING SUCCESS 104
CONCLUSION 112
HERE'S ANOTHER BOOK BY CLINT SHARP THAT YOU MIGHT LIKE 114
REFERENCES 115

Introduction

Are you looking for a way to take your fitness and sports skills to the next level? Then, wrestling could be the perfect choice. Its combination of strength, agility, and technique can provide an incredibly challenging workout while building skills to help you in other areas.

Wrestling is not merely a sport but a life-changing experience. It challenges individuals to push their limits physically and mentally, teaching discipline, perseverance, teamwork, and resilience. Wrestlers learn to navigate adversity, overcome setbacks, and find creative solutions to problems on and off the mat. This guide takes you through the basics of wrestling, from rules and skills to posture and balance to successful training techniques.

Beyond the competition, wrestling builds camaraderie and brotherhood like no other. It's a community of individuals united by their love of the sport and a shared pursuit of excellence. Wrestling isn't only about winning or losing; it's about the journey and the lessons learned along the way. You'll learn about penetration, lifting, attack and counterattack, reversal techniques, escape techniques, pinning combinations, and more. You'll learn about training at home and coaching youth wrestlers.

Wrestling teaches invaluable life skills and character qualities to carry throughout life. From discipline and perseverance to humility and leadership, wrestling instills valuable traits, making the participants better individuals. The bond between teammates is unbreakable, and the adrenaline rush of competing on the mat is unlike anything else.

Wrestling challenges people physically and mentally, pushing the limits and helping them discover their true potential. This book explores all these aspects and more.

Navigating it can be overwhelming if you're new to the wrestling world. The sport's intensity, the seemingly endless rules and regulations, and the sheer physicality can be intimidating. But don't let that deter you because once you dive in, the rewards are endless. A sense of discipline and harmony permeates every aspect of wrestling, from training to competition. In addition, the personal growth and confidence you gain from pushing yourself to your limits are invaluable. The road is sometimes challenging, but the payoff is worth it. So, step onto the mat because the wrestling world is waiting for you with open arms and endless opportunities.

By the end of this practical and concise guide, you'll have a thorough understanding of the sport and all it entails. With an eye for detail and commitment to excellence, wrestling will make you a better athlete and person. From learning the basics to finding success at the highest levels, this guide has you covered. The world of wrestling is vast and incredibly rewarding. So, what are you waiting for? Take the plunge and let this book guide you on your journey.

Chapter 1: Why Should I Choose Wrestling?

Wrestling might be your new obsession if you're looking for a sport to physically and mentally challenge you. Not only does it require incredible strength and endurance, but it also demands mental toughness and strategic thinking. Wrestling is a great test of character. It teaches you to push through pain and adversity, never giving up when the going gets tough. Moreover, the skills you learn on the mat apply to all areas of your life. As a result, you gain confidence and discipline, which carry over into your relationships, academic pursuits, and career.

If you want to become a better version of yourself while having fun and making lifelong friends, choose wrestling. This chapter explores the origins, philosophy, and benefits of wrestling. It discusses how it compares to other martial arts and which techniques can be used for self-defense training. The chapter ends with advice for parents considering enrolling their children in wrestling. By the end, you should thoroughly understand wrestling and why it's so popular.

Introduction to Wrestling

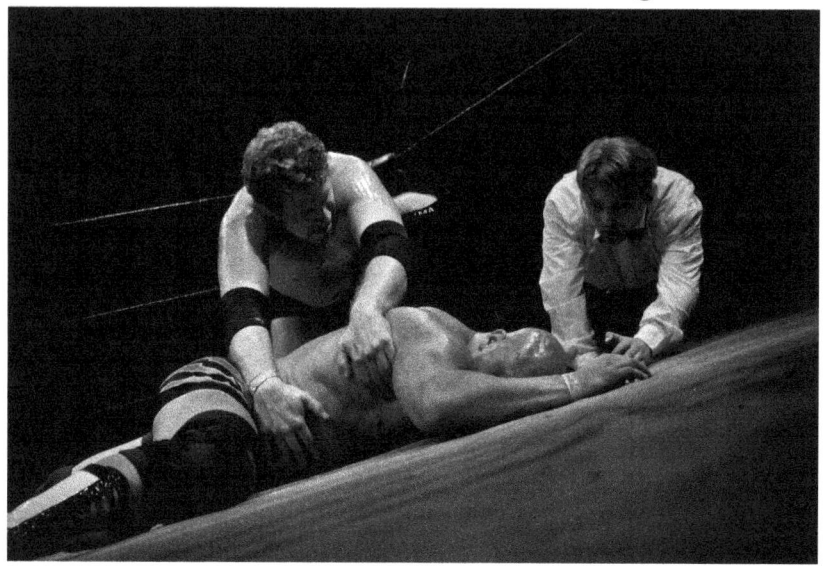

Wrestling is a sport where you try to pin your opponent to a mat.
https://unsplash.com/photos/o6h-CuvAypE?utm_source=unsplash&utm_medium=referral&utm_content=creditShareLink

Wrestling is one of the oldest and most popular sports in the world. It is a combat sport where two competitors aim to pin their opponent to the mat or force them out of the wrestling ring. Wrestling requires physical strength, agility, and strategic thinking. In addition, it's a sport that has evolved over centuries from its origins in ancient civilizations to modern-day Olympic competitions. This section explores the history of wrestling, its origins, and the philosophy behind this sport.

Origins

Wrestling has been around for over 15,000 years. It is believed to have originated in ancient civilizations such as Greece, Egypt, and Rome. Wrestling was popular in the earliest Olympic Games in Greece, where it was one of the five events in the pentathlon. In the Middle Ages, wrestling was a popular sport in Europe, with evidence of organized competitions in France, Germany, and England. Wrestling was also used as a means of self-defense and to prepare for hand-to-hand combat.

History

In the United States, wrestling became popular in the early 20th century with the formation of the Amateur Athletic Union (AAU) and the National Collegiate Athletic Association (NCAA). Collegiate wrestling became popular in universities, and high schools introduced it to their athletic programs. Professional wrestling emerged in the United States as entertainment, with staged matches and storylines.

In the latter half of the 20th century, wrestling became an international sport when the International Federation of Associated Wrestling Styles (FILA) formed and the inclusion of wrestling in the modern Olympic Games. Wrestling continues to be a popular sport worldwide, with millions participating and watching wrestling matches yearly.

Philosophy

Wrestling is more than just a physical sport. It's a mental and spiritual discipline. Wrestlers train their bodies to be strong and agile, developing a strong work ethic, perseverance, and mental toughness. Wrestling teaches skills such as focus, discipline, and self-control, which can be applied to other areas of your life. Wrestling also emphasizes respect for oneself and the opponent. In wrestling matches, competitors shake hands before and after the game, and sportsmanship is highly valued. Wrestling teaches humility and the importance of hard work and dedication.

From its origins in ancient civilizations to the modern-day Olympic Games, wrestling has evolved over the centuries. Wrestling is a mental and spiritual discipline teaching valuable life skills, such as self-control, discipline, and respect for self and the opponent. Whether you are a wrestler or a sports fan, wrestling offers a unique and rewarding experience.

Benefits of Wrestling

When people think of wrestling, they often picture two athletes grappling and throwing each other to the mat. While this is undoubtedly a big part of the sport, wrestling goes much deeper than that. Wrestling is a full-body workout requiring strength, agility, and endurance. It's a mental challenge promoting discipline, sportsmanship, and personal growth. This section explores the many benefits of wrestling and why it's more than just a sport.

- **Physical Strength and Endurance:** Wrestling is a physically demanding sport requiring strength and endurance. It engages every major muscle group, from the arms and shoulders to the

legs and core. Wrestlers must have cardiovascular endurance to sustain their efforts throughout a match. This intense workout helps wrestlers build muscle, burn fat, and boost fitness.
- **Mental Toughness and Discipline:** Wrestling isn't only about physicality. It's a mental game. Wrestlers must think on their feet, make split-second decisions, and maintain focus throughout a match. It requires mental toughness and discipline, positively impacting all aspects of a wrestler's life.
- **Teamwork and Sportsmanship**: While wrestling might seem like an individual sport, it requires a great deal of teamwork and sportsmanship. Wrestlers often train together and support each other through tough workouts and competitions. They learn to respect their opponents and demonstrate good sportsmanship, even in the heat of a match.
- **Community and Belonging:** Many wrestlers connect with their teammates deeply and develop lifelong friendships. Wrestlers can join clubs, attend events, and participate in philanthropic activities, helping them feel connected to something larger than themselves. As a result, the wrestling community is tight-knit, and many wrestlers feel a strong sense of belonging.
- **Personal Growth and Confidence**: Wrestling can help individuals grow and develop in numerous ways. It teaches resilience, perseverance, and the value of hard work. It promotes self-awareness and self-confidence as a wrestler sets and works toward achieving goals. Wrestling can be a transformative experience helping individuals become their best selves.

The benefits of wrestling go far beyond the physical aspect of the sport. It promotes mental toughness, discipline, and sportsmanship while creating a sense of community and belonging. Wrestling can be an excellent option for individuals looking to grow, build confidence, and strive for their best selves. Whether you're a seasoned athlete or someone just starting, wrestling has something to offer everyone.

Comparing Wrestling with Other Martial Arts

Combat sports have been around for centuries and are enjoyed by people of all ages. As a grappling-based martial art, wrestling is a great way to improve your strength, agility, and coordination while gaining valuable self-defense skills. Numerous other martial arts, like Judo, Karate, Taekwondo, and Boxing, also promote these skills. While all martial arts are effective in their way, each has unique characteristics setting it apart from the others. This section compares wrestling with other martial arts, highlighting the differences and similarities to help you decide which is best.

Wrestling is a great martial art for people who enjoy physical activity and high-intensity workouts. Wrestling involves a lot of grappling and clinching techniques and is considered one of the most challenging contact sports. Wrestling generally focuses more on takedowns, ground grappling, and submission moves than other martial arts like karate or kickboxing. It is an excellent exercise to develop muscle strength, endurance, agility, and balance.

While wrestling is a close-contact martial art, Judo is a slightly less physically demanding and more defensive sport. Judo is a martial art using throws and trips to take down opponents. It is considered one of the best forms of self-defense, especially against larger or stronger opponents. Therefore, Judo is a great martial art for people with a different physical fitness level than that required for wrestling.

Boxing, another famous martial art, is a combat sport using striking techniques like jabs, hooks, and uppercuts. Unlike wrestling and Judo, boxing primarily focuses on punching, fast footwork, and evasion techniques. The sport is widely popular for its cardio and weight loss benefits and improves cognitive function and balance.

Taekwondo, a Korean martial art, is a combat sport emphasizing quick, explosive movements and high kicks. Taekwondo is all about dynamic activities. This art form has proven exceptionally effective in self-defense and has been accepted as a full-contact sport in the Olympics.

Comparing wrestling with other martial arts indicates that each has unique strengths appealing to different people, depending on their interests and physical abilities. Wrestling might be the best choice to improve strength, coordination, and grappling skills. Judo could be the best pick for a less rigorous, defensive approach to martial arts. Boxing and Taekwondo are kickboxing arts to suit individuals who want to rely on striking techniques more than grappling. Choosing the right martial art (for yourself) is best based on your interests, goals, and physical capabilities. Whatever you choose, regular training and hard work will undoubtedly lead you toward self-discipline, mental toughness, and physical achievement.

Including Wrestling in Martial Arts Training

Martial arts have been practiced for centuries and encompass many combat techniques enhancing physical strength, mental agility, and overall well-being. From karate to jiu-jitsu, each martial art style has its unique set of movements, philosophies, and strategies. Wrestling is a popular martial art that has proven itself as a highly effective combat and self-defense form. This sport originated in ancient times and required intense physical effort, discipline, and practice to master. This section explores the benefits of including wrestling in your martial arts training routine and how it can enhance your practice.

Improved Physical Fitness

Wrestling is a demanding sport requiring strength, speed, agility, and endurance. By including wrestling in your martial arts training, you challenge your body in new and demanding ways, significantly improving physical fitness. Wrestling builds core strength, improves balance and coordination, develops explosive power, and increases cardiovascular endurance. These physical attributes are crucial to excelling in martial arts and will benefit overall health and well-being.

One primary reason people practice martial arts is to learn self-defense techniques to protect them from harm in dangerous situations. Wrestling is a technique enhancing your self-defense skills, making you more confident in your ability to defend yourself. In wrestling, you learn to take down your opponent, control their movements, and leverage your body weight to gain the upper hand. These same skills can be used in real-life self-defense situations, making wrestling a practical martial art to learn.

Mental Toughness

In addition to physical fitness, wrestling develops mental toughness, discipline, and focus. The intense physical demands of wrestling require a high level of mental fortitude, staying focused, and the discipline to keep pushing past your limits. These mental attributes are critical to excelling in martial arts. Through wrestling, you will learn to overcome mental barriers, develop a strong mindset, and remain calm and focused under pressure.

Variety in Your Training

Adding wrestling to your martial arts training routine can add variety to your workouts and keep them exciting. Wrestling provides a different form of training than some martial arts, such as striking-based martial arts like karate or Taekwondo. Incorporating wrestling into your training routine challenges your mind and body in new and exciting ways and gives you a more comprehensive martial arts skill set.

Competitive Opportunities

Last – but certainly not least – if you enjoy competitive sports and want to take your martial arts practice to the next level, wrestling can provide many opportunities to compete. Wrestlers have numerous opportunities, from local to national championships, to showcase their skills and compete against other skilled fighters. Including wrestling in your martial arts training could open doors to new experiences and opportunities you might not have had otherwise.

There is no denying that martial arts are a fantastic way to stay physically fit, mentally sharp, and disciplined. Including wrestling in your martial arts training routine amplifies these benefits. You will improve physical fitness and self-defense skills, develop mental toughness, add variety to your training, and open doors to competitive opportunities. So, whether you are a seasoned martial artist or a novice, consider adding wrestling to your martial arts training routine and take your practice to the next level.

How Is Wrestling Practiced?

Wrestling is an ancient sport that has grown in popularity over the years. It is an intense and physically demanding sport requiring skill, agility, and power. But have you ever wondered how wrestlers train to achieve this level of competitiveness and toughness? Wrestling involves rigorous training in various techniques, strategies, and physical conditioning.

Training Locations

Wrestling practice typically occurs in a wrestling room or on a wrestling mat designed for wrestling. The sport requires a specific mat created with high-density foam and vinyl fabric. These mats are critical to ensure the wrestlers are not hurt during training, and they help absorb shock and reduce the risk of injuries. During practice, wrestlers will include strength and conditioning exercises in the gym, which involve weightlifting, conditioning drills, and cardiovascular exercises to increase endurance, agility, and strength.

Intensity

Wrestling practice is intense and physically demanding. Most wrestling teams practice regularly, often for several hours each day. The intensity of exercise increases as wrestlers become more competitive, and training often incorporates high-intensity workouts pushing wrestlers to their limits. Succeeding in wrestling requires dedication and persistence, and a willingness to drive yourself beyond your limits.

Techniques and Strategies

Wrestling is a strategic sport requiring a combination of physical and mental skills. During training, wrestlers learn various techniques enabling them to control their opponents. These techniques include takedowns, escapes, pinning combinations, and top-and-bottom wrestling. Wrestlers should study their opponents, analyze their strengths and weaknesses, and develop strategies to gain the upper hand. To stay on top of their game, successful wrestlers must consistently work on perfecting their technique.

Safety

Safety is paramount in any sport, and wrestling is no exception. During wrestling practice, coaches and athletes take every measure to avoid injuries. It includes proper warm-up routines, stretching exercises, and injury-prevention drills. During wrestling practice, coaches closely monitor athletes to ensure appropriate techniques to prevent injuries. Many wrestling teams require athletes to wear protective gear, including headgear, mouthguards, and knee pads.

Wrestlers undergo rigorous training in various techniques, strategies, and physical conditioning – all geared toward making the athletes more muscular and agile. The intensity during practice can be high, but coaches and athletes prioritize safety measures to avoid injuries. Overall, wrestling practice is a well-organized, well-structured system ensuring wrestlers are at their optimal training level and ready to compete, making it a test of physical and mental strength.

Styles of Wrestling

While wrestling may look like a simple sport at first glance, various styles have unique rules and techniques. This section discusses the different wrestling styles, their origins, and what makes them stand out.

Freestyle Wrestling

Freestyle wrestling is the most common wrestling form worldwide and is a regular Olympic event. This wrestling style originates from Great Britain and emphasizes fast and agile movements over brute force. Wrestlers can hold and catch their opponent's legs and use their arms to perform takedowns like Greco-Romans. The winner is determined by gaining the most points, scored through takedowns, reversals, and exposures.

Greco-Roman Wrestling

Greco-Roman wrestling is another wrestling form dating back to ancient civilizations. Named after its origins in Rome, this wrestling style does not allow below-the-belt attacks, leg holds, or using an opponent's legs. Instead, the focus is on upper body strength and throws using arms and shoulders. Although takedowns are legal, they should be executed while standing. Grip strength, explosive power, and proper leverage techniques are essential in Greco-Roman wrestling.

Folkstyle Wrestling

Folkstyle, or collegiate wrestling, is the style most Americans are familiar with. This wrestling form is popular in high schools and colleges in the United States and Canada, emphasizing takedowns and pinning. In folkstyle wrestling, takedowns are worth two points, while a pin is worth five. A wrestler wins if he pins his opponent's shoulders on the mat or gains the most points in the match.

Sumo Wrestling

Sumo wrestling originates from Japan and combines elements of wrestling and Japanese Shinto belief. Sumo matches are held in a circular ring, where the wrestler's objective is to push their opponent outside the ring or make them touch the ground with any part of their body except their feet. To compete effectively, Sumo wrestlers must maintain a strict diet and training regime to reach the required weight and size.

Beach Wrestling

Beach wrestling, known as sand wrestling, is relatively new compared to other forms. This style usually takes place on a sand surface and requires high levels of explosiveness and agility. In beach wrestling, wrestlers save time clinching and trying to get control. Instead, they immediately try to grip the opponent's legs or perform a throw. The match ends when the wrestler pins the opponent's shoulders to the ground.

Freestyle wrestling, Greco-Roman wrestling, collegiate wrestling, sumo wrestling, and beach wrestling each have specific rules, techniques, and traditions. In addition, each form requires a different set of skills, making every style unique and engaging.

Wrestling as a Sport for Children

Wrestling is a highly competitive and challenging sport requiring immense energy, endurance, and perseverance. In addition, the sport positively impacts physical and mental health, especially for children. This section explores the benefits of wrestling for kids and how to find the right environment.

Benefits to Kids

- **Physical Development:** Wrestling is an intense physical activity incorporating cardiovascular, muscular endurance, and muscular strength. It helps children build lean muscles, improve bone density, and promote flexibility. In addition, wrestling boosts children's cardiovascular health, leading to a healthy weight and an active lifestyle.
- **Discipline and Character Building:** Wrestling is more than physical activity. It teaches kids focus, discipline, and perseverance. Wrestling helps children learn to set goals and work hard toward them. It teaches them essential life skills, such as resilience, courage, and teamwork.
- **Mental Health:** Wrestling positively impacts mental health, especially for children. It boosts self-confidence, self-esteem, and self-awareness. Children who participate in wrestling feel more in control of their bodies and have a better self-image.

Finding the Right Environment

- **Age-Appropriate**: Finding an age-appropriate wrestling program for your kids is essential. Young children should start with basic wrestling techniques, while older kids can learn more complex moves. The program should be tailored to their physical abilities and experience level.
- **Safe Space:** Wrestling requires close contact with other wrestlers, which could increase the risk of injury. Therefore,

choosing a wrestling program that focuses on safety and offers protective gear is essential. Additionally, a good wrestling program should have experienced coaches who know how to teach wrestling safely.

- **Cultural Environment:** The environment in which your kids learn and participate is essential. Ensuring the program fosters a positive and supportive culture encouraging values like discipline, sportsmanship, teamwork, and respect is crucial.

Wrestling is an excellent sport for children providing many physical and mental benefits. It teaches skills like discipline, perseverance, and focus, which are essential in life. When choosing a wrestling program for your kids, find one that is age-appropriate, safe, and fosters a positive cultural environment. It's important to nurture future fighters and give kids a chance to experience this sport.

Children aren't the only ones who benefit from wrestling. Adults can improve their physical and mental health, too. Wrestling teaches you to be strong yet humble, to discipline yourself, and stay focused. It is a great way to release steam, gain strength, and practice balance. As with any sport, the best way to enjoy it is in a safe environment with knowledgeable coaches and teachers providing proper instruction. Don't let the intimidation of wrestling keep you from trying it. There are many different levels and styles, so whether you are a novice or have been practicing for years, there is something for everyone. So, grab your gear and join the fight.

Chapter 2: Basic Rules and Skills

Learning the basic rules and skills is crucial to success in wrestling. Whether a beginner or an experienced wrestler, understanding the fundamentals of the sport gives you a competitive edge. From basic moves like takedowns and pins to understanding the scoring system and rules regarding illegal activities, having a solid foundation of knowledge will help you outperform your opponents. Moreover, learning the basics will improve your technique and help prevent injuries on the mat.

This chapter discusses the basic rules and skills of wrestling so you can get off to a strong start in this exciting sport. It covers the fundamental laws of wrestling, basic skills, and techniques you should master. With this knowledge, you'll be well on your way to becoming an experienced and successful wrestler. The following chapters go into greater detail about specific skills and strategies. But, for now, let's look at the basics.

Fundamental Rules of Wrestling

At its core, wrestling is a fight between two athletes governed by rules to ensure fair play and protect the competitors' safety. This section looks at the fundamental laws of wrestling, including the match set-up, scoring system, and disqualifications and penalties. It'll give you a solid understanding of how wrestling works and what it takes to be successful in this thrilling sport.

Match Set-Up

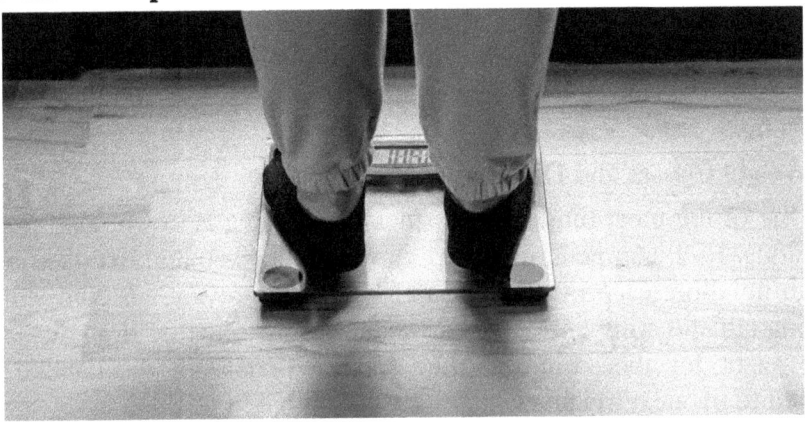

Wrestlers weigh in to determine the class they'll compete in.
https://www.pexels.com/photo/plus-size-woman-standing-on-scale-6551401/

Before a wrestling match begins, a few things must happen. First, the wrestlers must weigh in to determine which class they will compete in. Once they have weighed in, the wrestlers are called to the mat and introduced to the audience. Each wrestler takes their position on the mat, with one wrestler in the blue corner and the other in the red corner. Next, the referee signals the start of the match, and the wrestlers will engage in takedowns, reversals, and escapes to score points and win the game.

Scoring System

The scoring system in wrestling is relatively simple. Points are awarded for various maneuvers, such as takedowns, escapes, reversals, and pins. A takedown occurs when one wrestler takes their opponent to the ground and maintains control of them. An escape occurs when a wrestler escapes from under their opponent and breaks free from their grasp. A reversal occurs when a wrestler on the bottom manages to flip their opponent over and gain control. Finally, a pin occurs when one wrestler holds their opponent's shoulders on the mat for a specified period (usually two seconds) to secure the win. Points are also awarded for penalties and disqualifications.

Disqualifications and Penalties

Wrestling is a competitive sport, and sometimes tempers can run high. As a result, several rules govern disqualifications and penalties to ensure the competitors' safety and protect the sport's integrity. For example, wrestlers are not allowed to hit or strike their opponent with any part of their body and are not allowed to bite or pull hair. If a wrestler violates these rules, they can be penalized with a warning, a point deduction, or disqualification, depending on the severity of the offense. These rules are in place to protect the wrestlers and the sport of wrestling.

Weight Classes and Divisions

One of the most fundamental rules of wrestling is weight classes and divisions. Each competition features a weight bracket, and wrestlers must weigh in before each match. The weight classes provide fair competition among athletes with similar sizes, weights, and strengths. If a wrestler is overweight for their bracket, they can be penalized, disqualified, or moved to the next weight class.

Out-of-Bounds

Another essential rule of wrestling is out-of-bounds. The ring is known as the mat in wrestling, typically marked by an outer circle. If a wrestler steps out of bounds, they receive a penalty or forfeit the match. Therefore, staying aware of the mat's edge is vital, and ensuring your body doesn't cross over the line during a game is critical. Additionally, a wrestler must constantly maintain contact with the carpet and cannot purposely push their opponent out of bounds.

Time Limits

Most wrestling matches have a time limit, and understanding how it works is essential. Typically, high school and college-level matches are three periods, each lasting two minutes. If the match ends in a tie, the athletes go overtime and have one minute to win. During the overtime period, the first wrestler to score a point wins.

Scoring

The final essential rule of wrestling is scoring. Following the end of each period, the wrestler with the most points wins the round. If the points tally is tied at the end of the final period, wrestlers go into overtime. Points are awarded for different actions within the ring: 1 point for an escape, 2 points for a takedown, and 3 points for a combination of riding time and a near fall, where a wrestler almost pins their opponent.

The fundamental rules of wrestling ensure fair and safe competition for all participants. Mastering these rules is essential to becoming a successful wrestler. Weight classes, out-of-bounds, time limits, and scoring are vitally important to strategic wrestling. By understanding the match set-up, scoring system, and disqualifications and penalties, you'll tackle your opponents on the mat better and win more matches.

Basic Skills of Wrestling

Wrestling requires a unique combination of strength, agility, and balance. To succeed, you must develop fundamental abilities to overcome your opponent. This section discusses essential skills every wrestler should master to take their performance to the next level.

Balance

One of the most critical skills in wrestling is balance. A good sense of balance in wrestling allows you to maintain your position and keep your opponent from taking control. Good balance starts with proper body alignment and footwork. To improve your balance, work on your stance and positioning regularly. It includes practicing basic moves like the single and double-leg takedowns and challenging yourself with variations of those moves to improve your balance further.

Strength

Wrestling requires a lot of strength. You must apply force to your opponent and maintain your position effectively. Strength training is an essential part of a wrestler's training regime. It includes weight training and other resistance training to build overall strength. Focus on compound exercises, like squats, deadlifts, and bench presses, to develop functional strength. Working on grip strength is essential to help control your opponent and execute your moves more effectively.

Agility

Agility is the ability to move quickly and respond to your opponent's movements, another crucial skill in wrestling. Focus on exercises to improve your quickness and reaction time to develop agility. Agility ladders and cone drills can improve your footwork and reaction time. Plyometric exercises, like box jumps and lateral jumps, can help you develop explosive power and speed.

Mental Toughness

While not a physical skill, mental toughness is a critical attribute every wrestler must cultivate. Wrestling matches are mentally and emotionally strenuous events that test your limits. Developing mental toughness helps you push through the difficulties of a match and keep you motivated when training. To develop mental toughness, stay focused on your goals and visualize succeeding. Always remember that wrestling demands discipline, perseverance, and mental fortitude.

Endurance

Wrestling is an intense sport requiring significant physical endurance. Therefore, wrestlers need consistent cardiovascular training, such as running, biking, or swimming, to build endurance. The training improves your ability to sustain physical activity and last longer during wrestling matches. Additionally, it would be best to focus on developing strength and flexibility to maintain proper posture and movements during wrestling. Building endurance takes time and discipline but is an essential skill that can be the difference between winning and losing.

Mental Toughness

Wrestling puts a lot of pressure on athletes, and it's easy to become overwhelmed by stress and anxiety. Mental toughness helps you stay calm and focused during matches, perform at your highest level, and make better decisions. You can improve your mental toughness by setting realistic goals, working on visualization skills, and using positive self-talk. Learn to control your emotions, especially when things get tough. A wrestler who has honed mental toughness is better equipped to handle challenges that come their way.

Basic Knowledge of Strategy and Tactics

Wrestling matches require strategic planning and execution of moves. Knowing the basic tactics and strategies of wrestling is essential to succeed in the sport. Key strategies include controlling the center of the mat, maintaining balance, and staying aggressive. Knowing different techniques, such as takedowns, escapes, and pins, giving you an edge during matches is crucial. A good wrestler must understand how to anticipate their opponent's moves while avoiding predictable patterns. Work with your coach to develop a solid understanding of various strategies and tactics.

Self-Confidence

Wrestling is a one-on-one sport requiring you to trust your abilities and skills. Self-confidence is vital to winning matches. You must be confident in your physical skills, mental toughness, and knowledge of the sport; it comes with practice and experience. To build self-confidence, focus on your strengths, analyze your weaknesses, and set achievable goals to improve both. It would be best to surround yourself with positive and supportive people who believe in you. Self-confidence helps you overcome adversity, leading to more success on the mat.

Wrestling is a challenging but rewarding sport, and mastering the fundamental skills discussed in this section will help you become a successful wrestler. Endurance, mental toughness, strategy and tactics, and self-confidence are critical aspects of wrestling to enhance your performance and lead you to victory. Remember, wrestling is a sport requiring dedication, hard work, and discipline, but the rewards are plentiful. So, keep working on your skills, stay focused, and always improve.

Tips for Wrestling Beginners

Wrestling is a physically demanding sport of endurance, strength, agility, and technique. It's a sport that challenges physical capabilities and mental toughness. If you are a beginner in the world of wrestling, here are a few things to consider.

- **Work on Your Cardio:** Cardiovascular endurance is essential in wrestling, as the sport requires maintaining high intensity for an extended period. You must train your heart and lungs to efficiently deliver oxygen to your muscles. Some great ways to improve cardio include running, cycling, swimming, and jumping rope. Incorporate cardio into your training regimen; you will last longer in matches.
- **Proper Nutrition:** Proper nutrition is crucial in any sport, and wrestling is no exception. As a wrestler, you must consume a balanced diet of proteins, carbohydrates, and healthy fats. In addition, eat plenty of fruit and vegetables. Avoid sugary and processed foods, which can affect your energy levels and hinder performance.
- **Master the Fundamentals:** Wrestling requires a strong foundation in the fundamentals. Learning the basic stances, shots, and takedowns is best. Spend time drilling these basic moves so that they become second nature. Once you have a firm grip on the fundamentals, you can move on to more advanced techniques.
- **Train with Partners of Different Skill Levels**: Training with partners of different skill levels challenges you substantially. For example, wrestling with someone better than you can hone your techniques while wrestling with someone less skilled refines

your moves. You can learn something from everyone, so feel free to step outside your comfort zone and train with different partners.
- **Stay Motivated:** Wrestling can be physically and mentally challenging, so it's essential to stay motivated. Set realistic goals and track your progress. Surround yourself with positive, like-minded individuals who will support and motivate you. Be bold and seek inspiration from top wrestlers, and always remember why you started wrestling in the first place.

Basic Techniques in Wrestling

Whether you're a casual observer or a serious athlete, wrestling is a fun, challenging, and rewarding sport. From the high school mat to the Olympic stage, wrestling demands a perfect blend of strength, speed, and technique. One of the most important things to remember when just starting in wrestling is to master the basics. You don't need fancy moves or intricate leg locks. Instead, focus on simple techniques that can significantly impact the mat. This section discusses some of the most fundamental processes in wrestling.

Stance and Motion

Before you can execute a move – at least *well* – you must master the basic wrestling stance, a balanced and athletic position. Start with your feet shoulder-width apart and your knees slightly bent. Your back must be straight, and your head should be facing forward. Keep your hands up and your elbows in. This position allows you to move quickly without being thrown off balance. Always keep your feet moving, shuffling from side to side, circling your opponent, and changing levels to keep them guessing.

Escapes

Escapes are key to getting out of challenging positions and avoiding being pinned. The most basic escape is the stand-up, pushing off the mat with your hands and rolling onto your feet. From there, you can escape your opponent's grip, return to your feet, and start again. Another good escape is the hip heist, using your hips to create space and twist out of a hold. But, again, remember to keep your movements quick and dynamic and keep your opponent from getting too comfortable on top of you.

Reversals

Reversals are about turning the tables on your opponent, taking what they had, and making it your own. The simplest reversal is the switch. It includes turning into your opponent and rolling them onto their back. This move can be very effective if executed smoothly and quickly. Another classic reversal is the Peterson roll. This move requires more finesse and practice but can be versatile if mastered. Again, it would be best to bait your opponent to overcommit before flipping them over onto their back or exposing their shoulders.

By learning the basics of wrestling, the stance, motion escape, and reversals, you'll quickly develop your skills and become a more confident wrestler. Remember, keep your movements quick and fluid and your chin up. Wrestling is about challenging yourself, pushing your limits, and having fun. Whether a beginner or experienced wrestler, the basics are always the building blocks of success.

Takedowns

Takedowns are essential to wrestling, earning points and giving a wrestler an advantage. The objective is to bring your opponent down to the mat by taking them off their feet. Several takedown approaches include the single leg, double leg, and fireman's carry. Mastering one or two takedown techniques through repetition and practice is essential for success. The method requires studying your opponent's movements and anticipating their next move. Once you have the opponent on the mat, the next step is to initiate a pinning combination.

Pinning Combinations

Pinning combinations are the cornerstones of wrestling. Knowing different techniques to score points is essential once your opponent is on the mat. Various pinning techniques include a cradle, half Nelson, and chicken wing. A good wrestler should have a repertoire of several pinning combinations to surprise their opponent and score essential points. Depending on the situation, pinning techniques can be executed after a takedown or from the standing position. A wrestler's ability to read an opponent and identify their weaknesses is essential to implement these techniques successfully.

Practice

To master the basics of wrestling, you must practice consistently with a positive attitude to enable you to learn from your mistakes. The repetitive drills help perfect your moves and build muscle memory, increasing your technical abilities and efficiency. Watching and learning from other wrestlers and coaches is an excellent way to learn.

Conditioning

Last, conditioning, including strength training and cardio, is essential to building endurance and keeping up with the physical demands of wrestling. Therefore, a good wrestler should have a balanced workout regime, including strength and cardio exercises, to build athletic abilities and resist fatigue.

Leg Riding and Control

Leg riding and control are fundamental techniques in wrestling. The first step is establishing control over an opponent's leg by wrapping your leg around them or hooking your arm under their leg. Once you have control, focus on maintaining pressure and balance. Keep your weight on your opponent to prevent them from escaping. To ride the legs effectively, use ankle and hip control. Keep your opponent's ankle tucked tightly against your body, and use your hip to apply pressure, making it difficult for your opponent to escape or maneuver their body. From here, you can transition to various moves, like a tilt or a turn.

Finishes

Once you've gained control over your opponent, it's time to execute a finish. The most common finishes in wrestling are pins, takedowns, and turns. Each requires different techniques and strategies. To perform a pin, your opponent's shoulders must be on the mat for two seconds. The easiest way to achieve this is to lift your opponent's leg and sweep their torso to the mat. Once your opponent is on their back, hold them down with your body weight and drive your shoulder into their chest.

Takedowns' objectives are to take your opponent to the mat. The key is to use your momentum and leverage to overpower your opponent. One of the most common takedowns is the double-leg takedown. It involves shooting quickly toward your opponent's legs, wrapping your arms around them, and lifting them off the ground. Turns are used to gain points by exposing your opponent's back to the mat, typically done from a top position. Use your weight and hip control to turn your opponent onto their back, then hold them down to secure the points.

Wrestling is a sport demanding physical endurance, mental agility, and mastering basic wrestling techniques. Takedowns and pinning combinations are fundamental skills every wrestler must know. Fundamental techniques help wrestlers establish and maintain a dominant position against their opponents. Refining essential wrestling techniques takes a lot of practice, persistence, and dedication. Building endurance is critical for a wrestler to survive the rigors of the sport, and a balanced workout regime, including strength and cardio exercises, is essential. With a positive attitude and regular practice, mastering these basic techniques will help you become a better wrestler.

Chapter 3: Posture and Balance

Posture and balance are the most critical factors in achieving success on the mat. Maintaining good posture ensures you can generate maximum power and leverage in your moves while preventing injury. Meanwhile, having excellent balance allows you to stay in control of your opponent, preventing them from gaining the upper hand. But mastering these skills is a challenging feat. It takes time, dedication, and a willingness to push yourself to your limits.

With patience and practice, you'll improve every day. This chapter provides an in-depth look at the importance of posture and balance in wrestling and the exercises that develop them. It explores how they positively affect your everyday life. You'll observe the mistakes people often make in posture and balance and how they affect your health, and you'll understand how posture and balance are essential to success in wrestling.

Posture and Balance in Wrestling

Wrestling is an intense and physically demanding sport requiring agility, strength, and skill. Wrestlers must learn to maintain proper posture and balance to excel in this sport. Good posture and balance can mean the difference between winning and losing a match. This section explores the importance of maintaining proper posture and balance in wrestling.

Importance of Good Posture

Posture is critical to the performance of a wrestler. Proper posture helps wrestlers maintain balance, prevent injury, and control their opponents. Wrestlers with good posture can remain in a more advantageous and stable position, giving them a tactical advantage. Wrestlers in good posture are less likely to suffer from injuries like strains and sprains. Also, proper posture ensures wrestlers can generate maximum power and leverage from their moves.

Benefits of Good Balance

Balance is another crucial factor in wrestling. Wrestlers with good balance can move quickly and fluidly, helping them evade the opponent's attacks and launch counter-offensive moves. Good balance allows wrestlers to maintain control when grappling on the mat. Additionally, a wrestler with good balance can use their body position to keep an opponent in place and avoid being pinned. Moreover, a wrestler with good balance is less prone to injury.

Working on Posture and Balance

Wrestlers can improve their posture and balance through targeted exercises. Strengthening the core muscles is critical to creating a solid foundation for good posture and balance. One exercise that targets the core muscles is the plank, which involves holding a push-up position for a specified time. Additionally, lunges can improve balance by strengthening the legs and hips. Resistance band exercises are practical for improving balance. For example, standing on one leg while holding a resistance band can develop balance and stability.

Good posture and balance prevent injuries, maintain control during matches, and create strategic advantages. You can achieve better posture and balance by incorporating exercises to improve your core and lower body strength and by maintaining proper positioning during games. The key is to be consistent and persistent in your training and to make good posture and balance a natural part of your wrestling technique. You will see the benefits and dominate your opponents with time and dedication.

Exercises for Good Posture and Balance

Maintaining good posture and balance during a match requires focus and awareness. Keeping the head up and the shoulders back is vital to maintaining good posture. Additionally, you must constantly be aware of your foot and body position for good balance. This section covers the essential exercises for improving posture and balance, which wrestlers should prioritize in their training routine.

Planks

Planks can be helpful for developing core strength.
https://www.pexels.com/photo/young-determined-man-training-alone-on-street-sports-ground-in-sunny-day-3768901/

Planks are one of the best exercises for developing core strength, which is essential for maintaining good posture and balance. They target all the major muscles in the core, including the abs, obliques, and lower back. To perform a plank, get into a push-up position with your forearms on the ground. Your elbows should be directly under your shoulders. Hold this position for 30 seconds to 1 minute, or as long as you can without losing form.

Mini-Band Walks

Mini-band walks can help improve balance and stability.

Mini-band walks are excellent exercises for improving balance and stability. They target the muscles in your legs and hips that control lateral movement, essential for maintaining a solid base in wrestling. To perform mini-band walks, place a mini-band around your ankles and stand with your feet shoulder-width apart. Then, take small steps to the side, keeping the tension on the band during the entire exercise. Repeat this action taking ten steps in each direction.

Lunges

Lunges can improve posture, balance, and leg strength.
https://www.pexels.com/photo/woman-in-green-sports-bra-and-black-leggings-doing-leg-lunges-999257/

Lunges are excellent for improving posture, balance, and leg strength. They work the muscles in your glutes, hamstrings, and quads – essential for maintaining a stable base in wrestling. For example, step forward with one foot and lower your body until your front knee is bent to a 90-degree angle to perform a lunge. Your back knee should be just above the ground. Repeat with the other leg.

Single-Leg Deadlifts

Single-leg deadlifts target your hips, hamstrings, and lower back muscles.

Single-leg deadlifts are a challenging exercise targeting your hips, hamstrings, and lower back muscles. They improve balance and stability, which is vital for wrestlers to maintain their balance while taking down opponents. Stand on one foot with a slight bend in your knee to perform a single-leg deadlift. Slowly lower your torso toward the ground while extending your other leg behind you. Keep your back straight and your core engaged. Repeat with the other leg.

Stability Ball Pikes

Stability ball pikes target your core, shoulders, and hip muscles.

Stability ball pikes are an advanced exercise targeting your core, shoulders, and hip muscles. They improve balance and stability, and overall body control. To perform a stability ball pike, start in a push-up position with your feet on a stability ball. Next, push your hips up toward the ceiling while bringing your feet toward your hands. Finally, slowly lower back to the starting position.

Benefits of Good Posture and Balance

Wrestling is one of the most physically demanding sports requiring strength, agility, and coordination. These skills are heavily reliant on posture and balance. As a wrestler, you understand the importance of these two components for performance in the ring. Additionally, good posture and balance are crucial for wrestling because they reduce the risk of injury and enhance overall performance. This section discusses the benefits of good posture and balance in wrestling and how to improve them to take your game to the next level.

Improved Technique

A wrestler's technique is the bread and butter of their game. You must have a proper foundation of posture and balance to execute techniques accurately. Good posture allows you to maintain a stable base while performing offensive or defensive moves. The right balance lets you adjust your weight distribution and movement to anticipate your opponent's next move. By improving your posture and balance, you'll be ready to execute your techniques effectively and react confidently to your opponent's moves.

Reduced Risk of Injury

Wrestling is a high-risk sport, often leading to injuries. Good posture and balance help maintain proper body alignment and reduce the risk of getting hurt. Correct posture keeps your spine in a neutral position, minimizing the strain on your back muscles and reducing the risk of back injuries. Proper balance allows you to distribute your weight evenly, preventing you from landing awkwardly and injuring your joints.

Increased Strength and Endurance

Proper posture and balance are essential for building strength and endurance during training. However, maintaining good posture and balance takes a lot of energy, especially during long wrestling matches. By practicing balance exercises and techniques, you develop core and leg muscles, allowing you to build strength and endurance. Additionally, improved endurance helps you stay focused and alert throughout the match, giving you a competitive edge over your opponent.

Better Movement Coordination

Wrestling involves a lot of quick and seamless movements necessitating coordination between your upper body, lower body, and core muscles. Good posture and balance improve your movement coordination by connecting all your muscles and allowing them to work together smoothly. Improved coordination enables you to move efficiently and quickly, putting less strain on your muscles and reducing fatigue.

Enhanced Mental Focus

Last, good posture and balance can enhance your mental focus. Wrestlers require a lot of mental toughness to excel in the sport. Practicing postures and balance exercises help you focus on your physical movements, clearing your mind of distractions. A focused mind keeps you alert, concentrated, and calm under high-pressure situations.

You must regularly improve your posture and balance to become a successful wrestler. Incorporating posture and balance exercises into your routine can enhance your technique, reduce injury, and develop strength, endurance, movement coordination, and mental focus. A well-rounded wrestling performance requires a strong foundation of proper posture and balance. With dedication and effort, you can unlock your full wrestling potential.

Mistakes People Make in Posture and Balance

Unfortunately, many wrestlers make common mistakes regarding posture and balance, leading to injuries and match losses. Ensuring your body is in the correct position, and your weight is evenly distributed is essential. Taking too wide a stance can impede movement and throw you off balance. Here are a few more common mistakes wrestlers make regarding posture and balance and how to correct them.

Hunching the Shoulders

One of the most common mistakes people make in wrestling is hunching their shoulders – hunching strains the neck and back muscles, leading to chronic pain and injury. Hence, keeping your shoulders down and your back straight when wrestling is essential. This posture prevents unnecessary strain on the shoulders and back muscles and maintains balance.

Leaning Too Far Forward

Leaning too far forward is another common mistake in wrestling and can lead to injury. When wrestlers lean too far ahead, they put a lot of pressure on their knees and are more prone to getting taken down. The best way to prevent this mistake is to maintain a balanced stance. Keep your feet shoulder-width apart and bend your knees slightly to keep your weight centered.

Lifting the Chin

Many wrestlers lift their heads and chin while wrestling, impacting their balance. This posture is more challenging to maintain eye contact with your opponent, making it harder to anticipate their movements. Instead, tuck your chin into your chest, lower your head, and maintain eye contact with your opponent. This sets you up for better balance and control of the fight.

Not Maintaining Strong Core Muscles

Another mistake people make in wrestling is not keeping their core muscles engaged. The core muscles are essential for good balance and proper posture. Wrestlers lose their form and become more susceptible to injury when they don't engage their core muscles. Focus on breathing and engaging your abdominal muscles throughout the match to keep your core muscles activated.

Allowing Overextension in the Legs

During wrestling, overextending your legs is a common mistake fighters make. This posture can make you lose balance and expose you during your opponent's attack. It can lead to injuries to your legs and joints. Instead, focus on keeping your feet hip-width apart and engaging the muscles in your legs to keep your balance. You will maintain better control of the fight and avoid unnecessary damage to your body.

By avoiding these common mistakes, you can perform at your best and reduce the risk of injury. Remember, maintain proper balance, keep your core muscles engaged, and watch your posture, and you'll be on your way to becoming a better wrestler.

Developing Posture and Balance for Wrestling

Good posture and balance allow you to maintain stability and control while executing moves in the ring. Good posture ensures your body is aligned correctly, reducing the risk of injury and increasing overall strength. So, to improve your wrestling game, building a solid posture and balance foundation is a must. Here are tips and exercises to help you achieve good posture and balance.

Practice Good Posture

The first step in developing good posture is to practice daily. For example, consciously stand straight, pull your shoulders back, and keep your head up. It helps build muscle memory to maintain good posture during wrestling matches. Also, practice good posture while sitting, walking, and sleeping. For example, standing or sitting with hunched shoulders or slouching leads to muscle imbalances and poor posture over time. Also, it is best to have a comfortable mattress and pillows that support your back to maintain good posture while you sleep.

Strengthen Your Core

Your core muscles are the foundation for your posture and balance. Strengthening them maintains proper alignment and stability during wrestling matches. Some exercises to improve core muscles are planks, V-ups, and bicycles. These exercises target your abs, lower back, and obliques – vital for maintaining good posture and balance.

Improve Your Balance

Having good balance is critical while wrestling. Luckily, you can do several exercises and drills to improve it. Start with basic balance exercises like standing on one leg or using a balance board. Once you've mastered these, move on to more advanced exercises like single-leg squats, lunge variations, and instability ball exercises. These improve your balance while building leg and core strength.

Work on Your Footwork

Footwork is another crucial aspect of good posture and balance. Quick and precise movements require a solid foundation to build upon, which usually comes from proper footwork. Spend time practicing basic footwork drills like shuffles, ladder drills, and sidestepping. Once you've mastered these, move on to more advanced footwork drills to simulate movements commonly used in wrestling matches.

Focus on Your Breathing

Breathing is often overlooked in posture and balance discussions, but it's a crucial piece of the puzzle. Proper breathing techniques allow you to maintain stability and control while performing moves and increase endurance. Practice breathing deeply and intentionally while working on your posture and balance exercises. Inhaling on the way up and exhaling on the way down benefits balance.

Whether a seasoned wrestler or novice, working on posture and balance is essential to your success in the ring. By practicing these tips and exercises, you can develop a stability and control foundation to execute your moves with greater precision and agility. Remember, work on your posture, core strength, balance, footwork, and breathing, and soon you'll see a noticeable improvement in your wrestling game.

Tips for Maintaining Good Posture and Balance During a Wrestling Match

Maintaining good posture and balance during a match is crucial, as it helps you conserve energy, avoid injuries, and ultimately win the game. You must practice good posture and balance regularly to stay in control and on top of your opponent during a match. Here are tips to help you maintain good posture and balance during a wrestling match.

Engage Your Core

Your core muscles stabilize your body and maintain good posture during a match. Engage your core by pulling your belly button towards your spine and keeping your back straight. It keeps you balanced and avoids getting thrown off balance by your opponent. The key is to keep your core muscles engaged throughout the match by continuously contracting your abdominal muscles.

Keep your Feet Shoulder-Width Apart

Having your feet shoulder-width apart provides a solid base for maintaining balance and helps you resist takedowns. Keeping your weight distributed evenly between both feet is essential to avoid being thrown off balance. If your opponent tries to push you, keep your feet firmly planted on the mat and resist their force. You'll better counter their moves if your feet are stable.

Stay Low

Staying low helps you maintain balance while executing takedowns and reversals. Keep your hips below your opponent's level to gain leverage and increase control. It helps you avoid getting taken down or reversed. If you're on the defensive, stay low and use your core to resist your opponent's force.

Maintain Open Hands

Open hands provide balance and a better grip. If your hands are closed, it's difficult to react quickly to your opponent's moves, and you'll get thrown off balance more quickly. If your opponent gets close enough to grab you, having open hands will give you the flexibility to adjust and counter their moves. Once you get into the habit of keeping your hands open, you can take advantage of opportunities to execute takedowns and reversals.

Bend Your Knees

Slightly bending your knees helps you maintain balance and react quickly to your opponent's moves. It lets you lower your center of gravity, making it more difficult for your opponent to lift you off the ground. The key is to keep your knees slightly bent but still have them straight enough to move quickly. Also, stay low and bend your knees even more when in a defensive position. It will give you more control and gain leverage against your opponent.

Keep Your Head Up

Keeping your head up helps maintain good posture and awareness of your surroundings. It is crucial in wrestling because you can anticipate your opponent's moves and react accordingly. The ideal position is to keep your chin up and your eyes focused forward. It helps you avoid getting taken down or thrown off balance by your opponent.

Practice Yoga

Regularly practicing yoga can improve your balance, flexibility, and posture. Yoga poses focusing on balance, such as Tree Pose and Warrior III, can be particularly useful for wrestling. Even if you only practice a few poses for five minutes daily, it can give you an edge over your opponents. The benefits will be even more significant if you practice regularly and for a more extended period.

Use Your Breath

Your breath is crucial in wrestling as it helps you stay relaxed and focused. Taking deep breaths throughout the match conserves energy and keeps your muscles loose. When you exhale, visualize the movement of your body as if you were executing a move flawlessly; it helps you focus on the task and maintain good balance and posture.

Maintaining good posture and balance during a wrestling match is crucial for success. By engaging your core, keeping your feet shoulder-width apart, bending your knees, keeping your head up, and practicing yoga, you can improve your balance and posture and become a better wrestler. Regularly practice these tips and watch your performance on the mat improve.

Chapter 4: Penetrating, Lifting, and Other Maneuvers

Wrestling is an intricate blend of agility, strength, and strategy. At its core, wrestling involves several moves, including penetrating and lifting, requiring takedowns, pins, and submissions. It's a thrilling experience keeping spectators on the edge of their seats, marveling at the wrestlers' strength, skill, and technique. The sport demands dedication, perseverance, and discipline to master, but it's also an excellent way to get fit and build self-confidence.

Whether you're a fan or a wrestler, there's no denying the thrill of executing a perfect maneuver on the mat. This chapter focuses on some of the most common and valuable maneuvers in wrestling, offering details for each move and cautionary advice to avoid physical harm. It explains the different levels of motion and what is essential to focus on. By the end of this chapter, you'll better understand how to execute these moves and why they are so important.

Penetrating

Penetrating is an essential skill in wrestling, where a wrestler creates a successful offense by breaking through their opponent's defense and gaining control. It requires a combination of technique, strength, and agility. This section discusses three penetrating techniques: push-through, step-around, and rolling. Each technique works differently based on the opponent's body movement, positioning, and timing. So, let's dive into the penetrating world and master the art of dominating the wrestling mat.

Push-Through Technique

The push-through technique is best when an opponent is standing upright.

Push-through is a technique where the wrestler charges forward with speed and aggression. The aim is to overpower the opponent's defense by applying firm pressure on the upper body. Here's how to perform this technique:

- Start with a low stance and your head level with the opponent's chest.
- Next, drive the shoulder into the opponent's chest and push with the lead leg.
- Follow through with the trail leg and get behind the opponent.
- Secure control by locking the hands or grabbing the waist.

The push-through technique is best when the opponent is standing upright or has a weak defensive posture. However, if the opponent anticipates the move, they can counter with a sprawl or a Whizzer.

Step-Around Technique

The step-around technique requires good footwork.

The step-around technique involves a circular movement to get around the opponent's defense and secure control from the back. It requires good footwork and timing to execute effectively. Here are the steps to perform this technique:

- Start by faking a shot or an attack to force the opponent to react.
- Step to the outside of the opponent's lead leg and circle.
- Keep the head low and wrap the arms around the opponent's waist.
- Finally, secure control from the back and bring the opponent down to the mat.

The step-around technique suits opponents with a solid upper body but weak lower body defense. However, if the opponent sprawls, the wrestler can switch to a single-leg takedown or transition to another technique.

Rolling Technique

The rolling technique is best used when an opponent has a strong stance.

The rolling technique is a unique way to penetrate the opponent's defense by using their momentum against them. It involves rolling over the opponent's body and getting control from the side. Here's how to perform this technique:

- Start with a collar tie or a wrist control to manipulate the opponent's movements.
- Drop the weight and roll over the opponent's back by tucking the head and shoulder.
- Flip to the other side and secure control by grabbing the leg or the waist.
- Drive the opponent to the mat or transition to another move.

The rolling technique is best executed when the opponent is expecting a standard attack, or they have a strong stance. However, it requires excellent timing and coordination to execute effectively.

Penetrating is a crucial skill in wrestling, giving a wrestler the upper hand in the match. The push-through, step-around, and rolling techniques are three ways to penetrate the opponent's defense and gain control. Therefore, it's essential to practice these techniques regularly and master the timing, footwork, and positioning. Remember, the key to successful penetrating lies in anticipating the opponent's movements, keeping the pressure on, and maintaining focus and discipline. With dedication and hard work, anyone can master the art of penetrating in wrestling and become a formidable opponent on the mat.

Lifting

Wrestling is a combat sport demanding strength, agility, endurance, and technique. Regarding technique, lifting is essential to the game. Lifting can help you take down your opponent, control the match, and score points. However, lifting is a challenging task and requires proper training and technique. This section discusses the three most effective lifting techniques in wrestling: hip heist, step-over, and rolling split. Also provided are tips to improve your lifting skills and avoid common mistakes.

Hip Heist

The hip heist is the most basic lifting technique in wrestling.

The hip heist is the most basic lifting technique in wrestling and involves using your hips to lift your opponent. To perform a hip heist, you must be in a low stance with your feet shoulder-width apart, hands on your opponent's back, and your head down. Push your hips forward and lift your opponent while turning to the side. It gives you the leverage to take control of the match and score points.

Step-Over

The step-over is effective when your opponent is in a low stance.

The step-over is another effective lifting technique in wrestling, especially when your opponent is in a low stance. To best perform this maneuver, step over your opponent's leg with one foot while grabbing their opposite arm to perform a step-over. Then, lift your opponent's leg in the air with your other hand and step forward with your foot. It will cause your opponent to lose balance, allowing you to take them down.

Rolling Split

The rolling split is an advanced lifting technique.

The rolling split is a more advanced lifting technique in wrestling and requires proper training and strategy. To perform a rolling split, grab your opponent's leg and pull it towards you while rolling onto your back. Then, split your legs and lift your opponent with your legs, causing them to fall onto their back. This technique requires a lot of flexibility and agility, but it can be a game-changer if appropriately executed.

Tips and Mistakes to Avoid

You must focus on your technique, strength, and flexibility to improve your lifting skills in wrestling. It's essential to practice with a partner who can give you feedback and help you improve your technique. However, you should avoid common mistakes, such as lifting with your arms instead of your hips, not using your legs to support your lift, and not keeping your balance.

Lifting is a crucial part of wrestling, and mastering the proper techniques gives you the edge to win matches. The hip heist, step-over, and rolling split are three effective lifting techniques to take down your opponent and score points. However, mastering these techniques requires a proper approach, strength, and flexibility. You can improve your lifting skills and become a better wrestler by practicing with a partner, focusing on your technique, and avoiding common mistakes. So, keep training and honing your skills. Remember, practice makes perfect.

Back-Stepping

One of the most crucial and fundamental techniques in wrestling is back-stepping. The back step move allows wrestlers to gain leverage, control, and score points against their opponents. This section discusses the three back-stepping maneuvers, including the crab walk, step-behind, and reverse rolling, and their applications in wrestling matches. Whether a beginner or an experienced wrestler, this section provides vital insights and strategies to improve your back-stepping skills and dominate on the mat.

Crab Walk

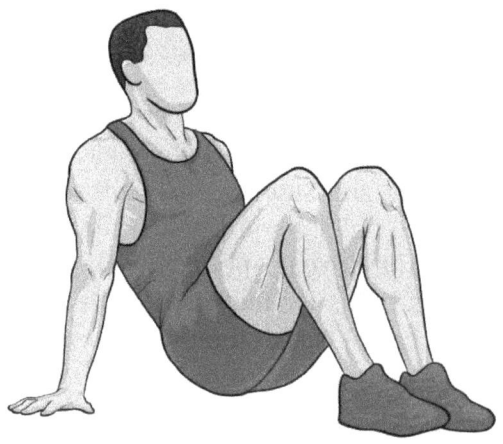

The crab walk allows you to move backward diagonally.

The crab walk is a back-stepping technique where the wrestler moves diagonally backward, stepping their foot across their opponent's foot. The wrestler's body lowers as they do, pressing the chest against their opponent's back. This move is beneficial when the wrestler's opponent is initiating a forward attack, and the wrestler wants to avoid the attack and gain leverage. The crab walk technique is a great defensive tool but can lead to counters, so it must be executed quickly and efficiently.

Step-Behind

The step-behind is another useful back-stepping technique by stepping diagonally backward while simultaneously stepping around the opponent's body. The wrestler places their foot behind their opponent's and controls their opponent's hips. This move is excellent for gaining an advantageous position over the opponent, especially when the opponent is attacking forward. The step-behind move is effective and leaves the opposing wrestler open to many other forms of attack, making it a versatile and effective technique to use in competition.

Reverse Rolling

Reverse-rolling can change the direction of a fight.

Reverse rolling is a back-stepping technique where the wrestler moves their body in a circular motion backward while stepping behind their opponent's leg. The wrestler turns their body so they face their opponent. In this position, they have a clear and dominant position to control their opponent. This technique is useful when the wrestler's opponent tries scoring points by grabbing their leg, allowing them to escape and attack from a position of dominance. When executed correctly, the reverse rolling technique is swift and dynamic for changing the direction of a fight, leaving the opponent vulnerable and lost.

Tips for Back-Stepping Moves

Back-stepping techniques are great tools but must be implemented with caution and precision. Here are some tips to help you improve your back-stepping techniques and make them useful in matches.

- **Practice Regularly:** Regularly performing back-stepping moves with the help of a training partner can help you confidently master the art of back-stepping.
- **Be Agile:** Back-stepping aims to dodge and avoid your opponent's attack, so it's essential to be light on your feet and nimble on your toes.
- **Control Your Opponent's Hips:** One of the most crucial aspects of back-stepping moves is to gain control of your opponent's hips. It helps you dictate the direction of the match and leverage against your opponents.
- **Use Combinations:** Mastering back-stepping moves is part of an excellent wrestler's arsenal. So, it's helpful to integrate this technique into various other methods, such as throws, takedowns, and submissions.

Back-stepping moves are fundamental skills every wrestler should master. The crab walk, step-behind, and reverse rolling moves are versatile techniques helping wrestlers avoid attacks and gain an advantageous position in matches. It's essential to practice and master these moves, along with sprucing up your agility and control. These moves are great techniques to use and integrate with other methods. Remember, a great wrestler requires patience, diligence, and strategy.

Back Arching

One essential skill in wrestling is getting up from the ground as quickly as possible, especially when your opponent is trying to pin you down. Back arching or kipping up is one technique to get up from the ground, but there are others, such as rocking up and springing up. This section explores the different methods of back arching in wrestling and provides tips to master them.

Kipping Up

A kip-up can help you get up quickly.

Kipping up is a widespread technique in wrestling, and many wrestlers use it to get up quickly from the ground. This technique involves rocking your legs to gain momentum and then thrusting your body upward to reach your feet. To perform a kipping up, you must start by lying on your back with your knees bent and your feet flat on the ground. Then, swing your legs toward your chest to generate momentum and kick them straight up while pushing your body off the floor with your arms. To master kipping up, ensure you swing your legs with enough power to generate the necessary momentum to get up. Also, you must push your whole body off the ground, not just your upper body.

Rocking Up

Rocking up is another famous technique wrestlers use to quickly get up from the ground. This technique involves rolling your shoulders off the ground to gain momentum, then bringing your knees under you to stand up. To perform rocking up, start by lying on your back with your knees bent, feet flat on the ground, and your arms by your sides. Then, rock your shoulders forward to create momentum, and bring your knees up while pushing off the floor with your arms. To master rocking up, roll your shoulders far enough to generate momentum. Also, push off the ground with your arms and keep your core tight to control your body's movement.

Springing Up

Springing up is a less common technique in wrestling, but it is an effective way to get up quickly. This technique involves springing off your feet and hands to reach a standing position. To perform springing up, start by lying on your back with your knees bent, feet flat on the ground, and your arms by your sides. Then, push off the ground with your feet and hands in one swift motion, bring your knees up, and stand. To master springing up, push off the ground with significant force, making the motion as fluid as possible.

Back arching is a crucial skill in wrestling, and mastering the different techniques can give you an advantage on the mat. Kipping up, rocking up, and springing up are three effective techniques wrestlers use to get up quickly. To master these techniques, practice the basics of each and focus on your form. Remember to swing your legs with enough power, maintain movement control, and keep your core tight. You can master these techniques and elevate your wrestling game to the next level with dedicated practice.

Different Levels of Motion

Understanding and implementing the various levels of motion is crucial to mastering wrestling. This section discusses the different levels of motion in wrestling, including high, medium, and low energy. By the end, you will better understand how to incorporate these levels of motion into your wrestling techniques.

High Energy

Fast, explosive movements characterize high-energy wrestling; this level of motion requires a lot of stamina and strength. High-energy wrestlers are constantly moving and attacking, rarely giving their opponents a chance to catch their breath – this wrestling style best suits agile athletes who can move quickly and easily. To incorporate high-energy wrestling into your technique, focus on initiating quick and explosive movements, like takedowns and reversals.

Medium Energy

The medium energy level is slower than the high energy level but requires significant energy and effort. In medium-energy wrestling, athletes constantly move but at a slightly slower pace. This level of motion is often used for strategic reasons, like setting up a takedown or waiting for the right moment to strike. Good medium-energy wrestlers can maintain a constant pace throughout the match, conserving energy for later rounds.

Low Energy

Low-energy wrestling is the slowest level of motion and is typically used for defensive strategies. This level of motion requires a lot of patience and skill, as wrestlers must move skillfully and avoid being caught off-guard by their opponent's attacks. Athletes control their opponent's movements while waiting for an opportunity to strike in low-energy wrestling. This level of motion is best suited for wrestlers with strong defensive skills who can maintain their composure even in high-pressure situations.

The different levels of motion in wrestling are crucial in every match. By mastering different levels of motion, wrestlers can strategically expend their energy, stay ahead of their opponents, and ultimately come out on top. Whether you prefer high-energy, medium-energy, or low-energy wrestling, understanding these levels of motion helps you become a more effective athlete. So, the next time you hit the mat, remember to incorporate these levels of motion into your technique and watch your performance soar.

Essential Focus Points

Wrestlers have to be mentally and physically tough to compete and be successful. Therefore, it requires strategy, practice, and discipline to master the techniques and tactics of wrestling. For a wrestler, the focus is critical and starts with understanding essential focus points. This section discusses three crucial focus points in wrestling: the center of gravity, balance, and kinesthetic awareness.

Center of Gravity

One of the most important focus points in wrestling is the center of gravity. Your center of gravity is the point in your body where your weight distribution is equally balanced. Having a low center of gravity is critical in wrestling. The lower you are, the harder it is for your opponent to take you down. Wrestlers must maintain this low center of gravity to stay balanced and prevent their opponents from gaining leverage. Therefore, focus on keeping your hips down and tight to your opponent to maintain an intense center of gravity.

Balance

Balancing your weight distribution is another crucial focus point in wrestling. You must remain balanced to execute moves and defend against your opponents. It requires core strength and ensuring your feet are correctly positioned. If you lose your balance, it will be much easier for your opponent to execute a move against you. Wrestlers work on balance by practicing moves requiring them to shift their body weight and maintain control. Focusing on balance allows you to stay in control during a wrestle.

Kinesthetic Awareness

Last, kinesthetic awareness refers to being conscious of your body's positioning and movement. For example, having control over the position of your body to execute moves to win wrestling matches is crucial. Knowing where your body is in relation to your opponent and the mat requires a specialized sense called kinesthetic awareness. This awareness can be developed through rigorous practice and improved by routinely working on drills and focusing on your opponent's movements.

By recognizing the essential focus points in wrestling, such as the center of gravity, balance, and kinesthetic awareness, wrestlers can position themselves to become better competitors. These three focus points are essential not only to master in wrestling but also in everyday life. Like in wrestling, maintaining a low center of gravity, balanced weight distribution, and awareness of movement allows you to progress and succeed in anything you set for yourself. So, focus, practice, and discipline as much as possible.

This chapter covered penetration, lifting, and other standard moves in wrestling. Knowing how to use these moves properly is essential for success on the mat, and mastering them requires focus, practice, and discipline. Awareness of your body's position and distribution of weight are crucial elements when executing moves. Additionally, you must understand the different levels of motion in wrestling, such as high, medium, and low energy. By mastering these levels of motion, you increase your mobility and agility on the mat, which ultimately helps you become a better wrestler. So, focus on the essentials and watch your performance soar.

Chapter 5: How to Attack and Counterattack

Wrestling is a sport necessitating skill and strategy to emerge as the victor. Wrestlers must be confident in their abilities to attack and counterattack effectively and know how to read their opponent's moves. It's about understanding their weaknesses and taking advantage of opportunities. Whether it's a takedown, pin, or submission, every wrestler has preferred moves they rely on. However, knowing how to counter these moves is crucial to stay ahead of the game.

With practice and determination, wrestlers can master the art of attacking and counterattacking, making them a formidable force on the mat. This chapter outlines some of the most common wrestling techniques to attack and counterattack and tips on avoiding mistakes and minimizing bodily harm. These techniques are significantly advantageous when attempting to gain control over an opponent. By the end of this chapter, you will better understand the different attacks and counterattacks in wrestling.

Unlocking the Power of Headlocks in Wrestling

Headlocks are a popular wrestling move.

Headlocks in wrestling are a popular move known for the effectiveness and ease with which they can be executed. However, not all headlocks are created equal. Some are more effective than others, and some can cause severe injuries if not done correctly. This section discusses the different headlocks, their benefits, and the correct ways to execute them. It provides tips on common mistakes and how to avoid injuries. So, let's dive into the world of headlocks.

Setting Up the Move

The first step in executing a successful headlock is correctly setting it up. It involves creating the correct position to perform the move. The position for a headlock typically starts with both wrestlers standing face to face. The attacking wrestler places their arm over the opponent's head and grabs onto their wrist or the opponent's arm. The wrestler must move their body close to the opponent, with their head tight against the opponent's head or neck. It creates a firm grip and position to execute the move.

Executing the Move

Once you have set up the move correctly, it's time to execute it. The wrestler squeezes their arm tight against the opponent's neck and twists their body to the side to apply pressure and maintain control. This should be done gradually without pulling the opponent too hard, as it could cause injury. The move puts immense pressure on the opponent's neck, making it difficult for them to breathe and escape if executed correctly.

Common Mistakes

One common mistake wrestlers make when attempting a headlock is pulling too hard. It can be potentially dangerous, especially if the opponent is unprepared for the move. Another common mistake is not setting up the move correctly, leading to losing control and a failed attempt. Avoiding being too predictable with this move so your opponent does not easily counter it is essential.

How to Avoid Injury

As with any wrestling move, it is vital to pay close attention to your opponent's body language and only perform moves you have practiced and are comfortable with. If you experience discomfort or resistance during the move, it's crucial to release the hold and try again later. Stretching and warming up is essential before attempting any wrestling move, including headlocks.

Headlocks are a decisive move in wrestling that can effectively control your opponent. It's essential to execute this move correctly, set it up properly, take it slow once you've grabbed the opponent, and avoid common mistakes. As with all wrestling moves, safety is critical. Always pay attention to your opponent's body language and avoid using too much force. With practice, you, too, can become a master of the headlock and a dominant force on the wrestling mat.

Master the Art of Executing Takedowns

Takedowns are necessary in combat sports.

Takedowns are an essential skill in martial arts and combat sports. It is a move that can instantly change the course of a fight and give you the upper hand against opponents. However, executing a takedown is more complex than it seems. It requires combining technique, timing, and strategy. Whether a beginner or an experienced fighter, this section will help you master the art of executing takedowns and avoiding injuries.

Setting Up the Move

Before executing a takedown, you must set it up properly. A takedown can be performed in many ways, from clinching, shooting, or catching the opponent off guard. One popular way to set up a takedown is using fake strikes or feints to draw your opponent's attention and create openings. Many experienced fighters use this technique in stand-up and ground positions. Other ways to set up takedowns include footwork, angles, or creating unbalanced positions to throw your opponent off balance.

Executing the Move

Once you have set up the takedown, it's time to execute it. A successful takedown requires good timing, technique, and speed. Some common takedowns include the double-leg takedown, single-leg takedown, and hip throw. To execute the takedown, you must ensure you're in the proper position and your opponent's weight is shifted in the right direction. Takedowns can be adjusted on the fly, so keeping your options open while executing the move is important.

Common Mistakes

Like other techniques, takedowns come with common mistakes that can harm your fighting performance. One frequent mistake is not setting up the takedown properly, leading to you getting countered or caught in a submission. Rushing the takedown or telegraphing the move can give your opponent enough time to defend and set up their counterattack. Other mistakes include overcommitting (rather than controlling the opponent's center of gravity) and failing to follow through with the takedown.

How to Avoid Injury

Takedowns are powerful and associated with high risk for you and your opponent. To avoid injury, first, ensure you execute a controlled move. Avoid using excessive force or momentum, which can cause serious harm to you or your opponent. Also, wear the proper protective gear, like a mouthguard and headgear. Last, if you're unsure about the appropriate execution of a takedown or are experiencing discomfort, consult a trainer or physician.

Mastering the art of takedowns is a crucial skill for an aspiring fighter. You can significantly improve your chances of winning a fight by setting up the move correctly, executing it with proper timing and technique, and avoiding common mistakes and injury. So, whether a beginner or an experienced fighter, remember these tips and continue practicing perfecting your takedown skills.

Mastering Submission Holds

Submission holds are the most effective way to dominate your opponent.
https://commons.wikimedia.org/wiki/File:Submission_wrestling.jpg

Have you ever been awed by how technical and precise some moves in professional wrestling are? Submission holds are one of these moves. This technique is one of the most complex and effective ways to dominate your opponent and win a match. However, submission holds can be intimidating, especially for beginners. This section walks you through the basics of submission holds and explores the steps to execute them flawlessly.

Setting Up the Move

Before anything, remember all submission holds start as a result of controlling your opponent's body position. You must put your opponent in a vulnerable position to set up a submission hold. Here's how you do it: you must create openings by being aware of your opponent's stance and looking for signs of weakness. When you notice an opportunity, seize it, and work your moves. If your opponent attempts to counter or resist the move, remain calm but assertive. Keep up the pressure until you execute the move. Setting up a submission hold requires skill, attention, and careful movements.

Executing the Move

After setting up the move, you must execute it efficiently, or you'll lose the match. Practicing submission holds repeatedly is the best way to perform the move flawlessly. Here are some steps to execute a submission hold: First, you must get close to your opponent. This way, you have a better grip to hold them down. Then, lock your grip and wrap your opponent's body parts, like the legs and arms, in your hold. Some submission holds require keeping a tight grip for a few moments, so be patient, focused, and always maintain your grip and balance. Last, ensure your hold is sufficient to force your opponent to tap out.

Common Mistakes

Some wrestlers make mistakes when executing submission holds, causing them to lose matches. Here are a few common errors in submission holds you can quickly correct:

- Not being patient enough to set up the correct position for the move can lead to counterattacks
- Not gripping tightly can lead to losing the hold and the match
- Losing focus controlling your opponent's body leads to them escaping the hold quickly
- Failure to observe balance can topple a wrestler and lead to a lost match

How to Avoid Injury

Injuries are commonplace in wrestling. However, you can reduce the risk of injuries by:

- Always correctly stretch before practice
- Wearing protective gear during training and matches
- Knowing your limits and not overstretching beyond your capabilities
- Seeking medical attention immediately if an injury occurs

Remember, a wrestler's overall health and well-being are essential to executing, winning, and enjoying the sport.

Submission holds are a great way to showcase wrestling techniques and win matches. To set up submission holds, keep an alert mindset, look for openings, and remain focused. Executing submission holds will require practice, patience, balance, and focus. By avoiding the common mistakes wrestlers make during submission holds, you can increase your chances of winning. Last, always take care of your health and well-being and seek medical attention when necessary. With these tips, you can master submission holds and become a successful wrestler.

Escaping Your Way to Victory

One of the most crucial skills in wrestling is the ability to escape. When caught in a hold or moved by your opponent, an escape can change the course of a match or prevent your opponent from scoring. This technique requires strength, flexibility, and quick thinking. This section guides you on recognizing an opponent's move, executing an escape, avoiding common mistakes, and preventing unnecessary injuries.

How to Recognize an Opponent's Move

The first step toward executing an escape is recognizing the hold or move your opponent has on you. It can be challenging since several moves in wrestling require different escapes. An excellent way to identify the move on you is to focus on the body part your opponent uses to hold or control you. For instance, if your opponent has a leg hold on you, try using various leg escapes to free your legs. Closely watching your opponent's movement will help you anticipate their subsequent actions, allowing you to prepare your escape.

Executing the Escape

Once you have identified your opponent's move, you must act fast to escape it. Being calm and level-headed is vital in this situation because you must think quickly. Common escapes include sit-outs, switches, and stand-ups, which require strength, flexibility, and technique. Additionally, practicing these moves beforehand increases your chances of executing a successful escape during a match.

Common Mistakes

One of the most common mistakes wrestlers make while attempting to escape is only partially committing to the move. If you hold back or hesitate, you will lose the upper hand, allowing your opponent to overpower you. Another mistake is relying solely on strength to escape rather than on technique. Using brute force works occasionally, but it will often tire you out faster, leaving you vulnerable to your opponent's next move.

How to Avoid Injury

The risk of getting injured is high in wrestling. Practice proper techniques and warm up before matches to prevent harm and injury. When executing escapes, avoid arching your back or twisting your neck, positions that could predispose you to injury. Last, knowing when to tap out is crucial. Although tapping out is a sign of weakness, saving your body from unnecessary harm is wise.

Escaping in wrestling is not merely a skill helping you to score points but a technique preventing your opponent from scoring. It takes patience, practice, and a keen sense of your opponent's moves. However, it can make all the difference in a match once mastered. Remember, stay focused, commit to the move, and prioritize safety first.

How to Master Reversals in Wrestling

To master reversals, you need to be able to anticipate your opponent's moves.

Wrestling is a highly technical combat sport involving muscle, speed, agility, and strategic thinking. One of the most critical aspects of wrestling is learning to reverse your opponent's move. This technique is essential for self-defense and can be significantly advantageous over your opponent. This section explores the art of reversals in wrestling, including recognizing an opponent's move, executing the reversal, common mistakes, and avoiding injury.

How to Recognize an Opponent's Move

Before executing a successful wrestling reversal, you must recognize your opponent's move. Some standard moves wrestlers make include a double-leg takedown, single-leg takedown, or a high crotch takedown.

The key to reversing your opponent's move is analyzing your opponent's position, leverage, and momentum. Learn the various wrestling techniques, drills, and sparring with experienced wrestlers.

Executing the Reversal

Once you recognize your opponent's move, timing the reversal execution is essential. Several reversals in wrestling include sit-out and switch reversal, Granby Roll reversal, hip-heist reversal, and Whizzer-based reversal. To perform a reversal, you must use your strength, speed, and agility to counter your opponent's momentum. Timing and precision are crucial to executing a successful reversal. It takes practice and training to master the art of reversals, so don't get discouraged if you struggle initially.

Common Mistakes

Even experienced wrestlers make mistakes with reversals. One of the common mistakes is forcing a reversal before the right moment. Another mistake is not following through on the reversal, leaving you open for a counterattack. Last, wrestlers might use too much force and injure their opponents, resulting in disqualification. Understanding the rules and regulations of wrestling to avoid penalties or injuries is essential.

How to Avoid Injury

Last, staying safe and avoiding injury when executing a reversal is essential. It involves proper technique, strength training, nutrition, and injury prevention strategies. Before performing a move, stretch and warm up your muscles to prevent sprains and strains. Furthermore, always listen to your body and communicate with your coach if you feel pain or discomfort. Wrestling is a physically demanding sport, and caring for your body to perform at your best is crucial.

Reversals are one of the essential techniques in wrestling, and mastering them can give you a significant advantage over your opponent. To execute a successful turnaround, you must recognize your opponent's move, analyze their position and leverage, and move with precision and timing. Avoid common mistakes like forcing the reversal too early or failing to follow through. Last, stay safe and avoid injury by following proper wrestling techniques, strength training, and injury prevention strategies. You can dominate the wrestling mat with practice and dedication and become a formidable opponent.

Effectively Counter Your Opponent's Move

You need to be able to counter your opponent's moves quickly.

As a wrestler, you aim to pin your opponent or score more points than them. However, you can only achieve these goals by reacting quickly to your opponent's moves and counters. This section discusses how to recognize your opponent's move, execute the counter, common mistakes to avoid, and techniques to prevent injury.

How to Recognize an Opponent's Move

The key to countering your opponent's move is to recognize it early. Therefore, it's crucial to have a good understanding of wrestling basics. Study your opponent's moves closely during the match by observing their positioning and movements. Pay attention to the subtle changes in their stance or body position, as these can indicate what move they are preparing to execute. Some wrestlers are known for their signature moves, so watch videos of their matches to familiarize yourself with their wrestling style. It helps you anticipate and counter their moves and prepare for their technique before the game.

Executing the Counter

Executing the counter requires quick reflexes, precise timing, and technique. Your countermoves depend on your opponent's moves, position, and wrestling style. A standard countermove is a "switch," where you quickly shift your position to reverse the move your opponent just executed. Another technique is a "roll-out," where you use your momentum to roll out of your opponent's hold and control the match. Once you have identified the move your opponent is attempting, execute the counter immediately. Being confident and decisive while performing the counter is essential, as hesitation can give your opponent an advantage.

Common Mistakes

While countering an opponent's move can be exciting and rewarding, it can also result in injury if not executed correctly. Wrestlers' mistakes while countering include poor timing, improper technique, and lack of focus. These mistakes lead to losing control of the match and allowing the opponent to capitalize on the error. To avoid making these mistakes, you must stay focused and patient. Remain in control of the situation and never panic, as this can lead to rushed or improper technique. Instead, take your time to execute the counter with the proper technique and timing.

How to Avoid Injury

Prioritizing your safety while executing counters is essential. Many injuries, such as sprains, fractures, and dislocations, result from countering. To avoid these injuries, you must warm up before the match, use proper technique, and keep your body limber. Another important tip is gradually increasing the practice's intensity to avoid overworking and straining your muscles. If you feel muscle or joint pain or discomfort, immediately stop and seek medical attention.

To become a successful wrestler, you must master the art of attacking and countering your opponent's moves. It includes recognizing your opponent's move, executing the strategy correctly, avoiding common mistakes, and prioritizing safety. This chapter covered tips and techniques to help you develop your skills as a wrestler. Remember, practice makes perfect, so keep practicing and improving your skills until you reach your goals.

Chapter 6: Reversal Techniques

As a wrestler, there's nothing more satisfying than landing in a tricky situation and executing a perfect reversal. You can transform what looked like a surefire defeat into a glorious triumph with the proper techniques. Reversal moves take different forms, from using your opponent's momentum against them to using your strength to flip the situation in your favor. Whatever the tactic, the key is to be confident in your ability to pull it off.

Building your arsenal of reversal techniques is essential to becoming a force to be reckoned with on the mat. So, get ready to enhance your wrestling skills and dominate your opponents. This chapter explores the reversal maneuvers, from basic switching techniques to more advanced offensive counters. It explores strategies for analyzing your opponent and gaining the upper hand.

Switching Maneuvers

Wrestling is about overpowering your opponent and being agile and quick in your movements. One critical factor in wrestling is switching to a favorable position when the opponent has caught you in a compromising position. Switching maneuvers helps wrestlers get out of holds and locks and gain control of the match. This section explores the different switches and their applications.

What Is the Switch?

Switching in wrestling means changing your body position from one hold or move to another. It allows wrestlers to break free from their opponents' grip and gain control. A switch can also be used to counterattack or execute a move. One of the most common switches in wrestling is the "sit out" switch. The move requires the wrestler to sit on their hips while pulling their opponent toward them and shifting their weight. The switcher shifts and takes control from behind as the opponent moves forward.

Reversing from Body Locks

The body lock is a common maneuver where the opponent wraps their arms around the wrestler's waist and shoulders, making it difficult to move. Wrestlers can use the "hip heist" switch to escape from this grip. In this maneuver, the wrestler drops their hips to the ground while pulling the opponent toward them. As the opponent falls forward, the wrestler shifts their weight and gains a favorable position to attack. The hip heist switch can also be used to counterattack.

Reversing from Backbreaker Holds

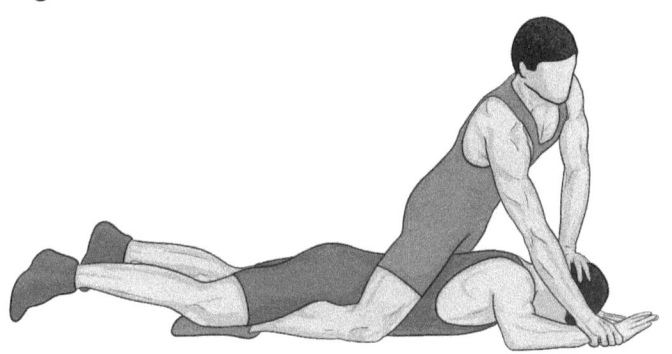

The grapevine switch helps you gain an advantage.

The backbreaker hold is a painful move putting pressure on the wrestler's spine and neck. However, wrestlers can use the "grapevine" switch to escape from this hold. In this maneuver, the wrestler loops their leg around the opponent's leg and twists their body, applying pressure to the opponent's knee and ankle. The grapevine switch is an effective maneuver to escape from the backbreaker hold and take control of the match.

Reversing from Chokeholds

A headlock switch can help you gain control.

The chokehold is a dangerous maneuver restricting the airflow to the wrestler's lungs and brain. Wrestlers can use the "headlock" switch to escape from this hold. In this maneuver, the wrestler wraps their arm around the opponent's neck, bringing their weight down. As a result, the opponent's grip loosens, allowing the wrestler to shift their weight and gain control. The headlock switch is an effective maneuver to escape from chokeholds and take control of the match.

Reversing from Pin Holds

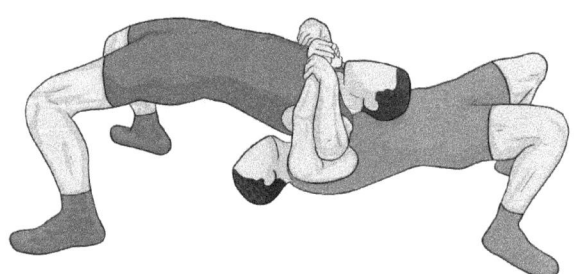

A bridge switch will help you reverse a pin hold.

The pin hold is when the opponent tries to trap the wrestler's shoulders on the mat for a count of three. Wrestlers can use the "bridge" switch to escape from this hold. In this maneuver, the wrestler shifts their weight onto their feet and flips their body onto their shoulders, lifting their opponent's weight off them. The wrestler shifts the weight onto their feet and gains a favorable position to attack. The bridge switch is an effective way to escape from the pin holds and take control of the match.

Switching maneuvers are a critical aspect of wrestling. They can change the outcome of a match and give the wrestler an advantage. Understanding the different switches and their applications helps wrestlers improve their skills and technique.

Transitional Maneuvers

Wrestlers are always looking for ways to outsmart their opponents in a match. The ability to seamlessly transition from one move to another is crucial for a wrestler to gain an advantage over their opponent. Transitional moves are like a bridge between different wrestling techniques that, when executed correctly, can make a significant difference in the outcome of a match.

This section discusses three transitional maneuvers to make you a better wrestler. These moves include the reversal to bridge, the roll-through escape, and the momentum to reverse. Each move requires precision and timing but can be mastered with focused practice.

Reversal to Bridge

The reversal to bridge is a great transitional move to counter an opponent's takedown attempt. Get into a seated position with your opponent on top of you and pin one of your shoulders to the mat. From here, push upward with the shoulder not pinned while simultaneously arching your back to roll your opponent over your body and onto their back.

You can bridge up and attack once your opponent is on the mat. Timing is crucial to execute this move successfully. You should initiate the move as soon as you feel your opponent's grip loosen, even a little. It helps move your head toward the unpinned shoulder to give yourself more leverage.

Roll-Through Escape

A roll-through escape will help you escape a side control.

The roll-through escape is another tremendous transitional move helping you escape your opponent's side control. Create space between you and your opponent. Next, turn onto your side, facing away from your opponent's chest, and pull your knee toward your chest while reaching your opposite hand toward your ankle. Use this momentum to roll onto your back and slide your knee toward your opponent.

Once you are in a more favorable position, you can attack. The key to this move is using your momentum and staying relaxed. The roll should be smooth and flowing, almost like a dance. It's essential to keep your movements fluid and controlled so you don't give your opponent opportunities to capitalize.

Using Momentum to Reverse

The momentum to reverse is a great transitional move to counter an opponent's attack. Get into a defensive position and wait for your opponent's attack. As they come toward you, use their momentum against them by sidestepping and pulling them forward, causing them to lose balance. Then, use your momentum to reverse the position and attack. This move requires excellent timing and awareness. It's crucial to know when your opponent is committed to an attack and to have the reflexes to react quickly. Stay low and relaxed and use your opponent's force against them to gain the upper hand.

Transitional maneuvers are an essential aspect of wrestling, giving you a strategic advantage over your opponent. The three moves discussed in this section, the reversal to bridge, the roll-through escape, and the momentum to reverse, are effective transitional moves helping you become a better wrestler.

Offensive Maneuvers

Whether a beginner or seasoned wrestler, learning offensive maneuvers can give you the edge to dominate your opponents, this section discusses three effective offensive maneuvers wrestlers use to gain an advantage in matches. These maneuvers include using an opponent's momentum against them, performing reversal sweeps and slams, and executing reversal counters.

Using the Opponent's Momentum against Them

The first offensive maneuver is using an opponent's momentum against them. This technique requires paying close attention to your opponent's movements and anticipating their next move. The aim is to use your opponent's energy to your advantage by redirecting it and taking them down. For example, if your opponent charges forward, step aside, grab their arm, and use their momentum to toss them over your shoulder. This move is called a hip toss.

Another move using this technique is the arm drag. Grab your opponent's arm and pull it past you. Then, as they move forward, you step aside and use their momentum to twist their body and take them down.

Reversal Sweeps and Slams

The second offensive maneuver is the reversal sweep and slam. This technique counters your opponent's takedown attempt by quickly transitioning into your takedown. For example, if your opponent goes for a single-leg takedown, you can quickly shift your weight and use a hip toss to take them down. This move requires a lot of speed and balance, but it can be devastating when executed properly. Another move using this technique is the arm drag takedown. In this move, grab your opponent's arm and use their momentum to throw them to the ground.

Reversal Counters

The third offensive maneuver is the reversal counter. This move requires anticipating your opponent's takedown attempt and using it against them. For example, if your opponent goes for a double-leg takedown, sprawl and use their momentum to take them down. This move is called a sprawling counter, one of the most effective moves in wrestling. Another move using this technique is the switch. Start on your back and use your leg to trap your opponent in this move. Then, as they move forward, quickly roll over and take them down.

Offensive maneuvers are essential in wrestling. Using an opponent's momentum against them, performing reversal sweeps and slams, and executing reversal counters are three effective ways to dominate the sport. The key to mastering these maneuvers is to practice them regularly and pay close attention to your opponent's movements. By incorporating these offensive techniques into your wrestling arsenal, you'll be well on your way to becoming a dominant wrestler.

Reversal Strategies

Wrestling, the oldest sport in the world, is more than just a competition of physical strength. It's a game of intelligence and strategy where the best wrestlers always watch their opponent's moves. When in the middle of a match, it's essential to be calm and patient, whether on top or bottom. Reversals can take you from being the underdog to becoming a winner in no time. By developing solid reversal strategies, you can swiftly seize control, leaving your opponent confused and stressed. This section explores the art of reversal in wrestling and three essential techniques to master it.

Mastering the Basics

The first step to mastering the art of reversal is learning the basics. A solid understanding of the fundamental movements and techniques, such as hip heist, Granby Roll, switch, and sit out, are the cornerstones to developing an effective reversal strategy. Practice these basics on a mat daily. Reversals require lightning-fast reaction and timing, and by ensuring these movements become second nature, you will have a winning edge. Moreover, it's essential to work on your grip strength. A firm grip will help you control the opponent throughout the match.

Developing Counterattacks

A counterattack is an offensive move to deflect and redirect the opponent's aggression or attack. Developing these counterattacks is highly effective during a wrestling match. First, familiarize yourself with your opponent's moves, anticipate their next steps, and prepare your counterattack. Counterattacks, like the Peterson and Granby rolls, are examples of effective retaliation moves to learn.

Work on Timing and Execution

Timing is significantly vital in wrestling. The same goes for reversal strategies. The wrestler who can quickly switch from defense to offense will most likely win. When targeting a reversal, excellent timing and execution to make it successful are essential. Be patient, anticipate your opponent's moves, and select the most effective reversal strategy at the right time. Remember, timing is everything.

Developing Mental Toughness

Good wrestlers possess outstanding mental toughness – they don't get affected by their opponent's moves. Instead, they use it to their advantage. As a result, they are calm and composed, even under pressure, and can quickly decide during matches. To develop mental toughness, you must keep practicing and build confidence. Participating in wrestling tournaments and facing tough opponents is a great way to gain experience and build mental strength.

Analyzing Your Opponent

Wrestling demands an assessment of your opponent before a move can be made. Wrestlers must leverage their strengths and exploit their opponent's weaknesses to gain advantage. Therefore, it would be best to learn your opponent's movements, timing, and tendencies to plan your moves correctly. Analyzing your opponent is critical to winning in wrestling. This section explains some essential tips to help you succeed on the mat.

Identifying Weaknesses

The first step to successfully analyzing your opponent is identifying their weaknesses. Every wrestler has their strengths and weaknesses, including your opposition. Take note of how they move, their body type, position, and style. You can tell if they struggle with takedowns, escapes, or pins. Understanding their weaknesses helps you plan strategic maneuvers targeting these vulnerabilities. Then, build your game plan based on your opponent's weaknesses and aim to outsmart them.

Looking for Opportunities

When you identify your opponent's weaknesses, look for opportunities to apply your strengths. Observe your opponent during warm-ups or at the start of the match. Study their footwork and timing to predict their moves and plan countermoves. Understand that opportunities arise anytime during a match, so be alert and ready to adjust your game plan.

Using Defense Tactics

Learning to defend yourself against your opponent's attacks is essential. Protecting yourself is as crucial as executing takedowns. Study your opponent's technique and learn to identify when you are vulnerable. Your opponent will likely take advantage of observed weaknesses, so practice countering their attacks and staying on the offense.

Mustering Stamina

Stamina is essential for wrestlers hoping to win. Your ability to perform at peak levels for the entire game relies heavily on your fitness levels. A lack of endurance and strength will almost immediately ruin your chances of winning. Therefore, keep up your workouts and training routines to sustain your energy and focus for the entire match.

Reversals are essential for a wrestler's game plan; it requires a comprehensive strategy to master. However, with practice, a solid foundation, developing counterattacks, and a great sense of timing and execution, you can outsmart your opponent quickly. Work on perfecting your fundamental movements, study your opponent's moves, familiarize yourself with your counterattack techniques, and build physical and mental toughness. Remember, every second of a match is an opportunity; with the right strategy, you can emerge as the winner.

Chapter 7: Escape Techniques

There's nothing quite like the thrilling intensity of a wrestling match. When locked in a grapple with your opponent, finding a way out is the only thing on your mind. Hence, the importance of escape techniques is paramount. These moves let you break free from your opponent's grip and gain an advantage. As a wrestler, mastering escape techniques is essential to come out on top. The best wrestlers can turn their opponent's momentum against them, using their body weight and leverage to gain the upper hand. But it's not only about raw power. It's about strategy, instincts, and quick reflexes.

With the proper escape techniques, anyone can turn the tables in battle and claim victory. This chapter covers various escape techniques and how to use them effectively. It explores defense techniques and tips on how to increase your escaping efficiency. So, if you're ready to step up your wrestling game, start mastering those escapes and show your opponents whose boss.

Top Position Escapes

Wrestling requires physical prowess, mental fortitude, and a good understanding of techniques. Whether you're a beginner or an advanced wrestler, mastering the various escape techniques to escape a tough spot is crucial. For example, your opponent catches you in a top position through a takedown or a pinning combination. This section looks at the top position escapes to regain control of the match.

Overhook Escape

Overhooks can be difficult to escape.
*daysofthundr46, CC BY-SA 2.0 <https://creativecommons.org/licenses/by-sa/2.0>, via Wikimedia Commons:
https://commons.wikimedia.org/wiki/File:Antonio_Thomas_with_armbar.jpg*

When your opponent has an overhook, it can be challenging to get away. The best way to escape an overhook is using the "Overhook Wrist Control" technique. First, move your arm under your opponent's arm and grab their wrist, giving you better leverage and control. Use your other arm to press down on their shoulder, twisting them toward the mat. Now, slide your body away and get into a neutral position. This technique helps you break free from your opponent's overhook and return to the game.

Underhook Escape

Underhook escapes are effective in taking down your opponent.

If your opponent has an underhook, you can use a few techniques to escape. One of the most effective escapes is the *Whizzer*. First, grab your opponent's wrist with one hand and their triceps with the other. Now, push their arm up and out while rotating your body away from them, creating enough space for you to get away and gain control of your position. Keep practicing this technique until you can do it effortlessly during a match.

Headlock Escape

Headlocks can quickly lead to a pin.

A headlock is a dangerous position that can quickly lead to a pin. If you're in a headlock, don't panic. Instead, use the "switch" technique to escape. Grab your opponent's elbow with one hand and their opposite wrist with the other. Now, roll toward their trapped arm and use your legs to create space. Once you're out of the headlock, get back on your feet and use your techniques to take control of the match. With enough practice, the switch technique will become second nature.

Bear Hug Escape

Bear hugs can be deadly if you don't escape.

A bear hug can be deadly if you don't know how to escape it. To escape the bear hug, first, wrap your arms around your opponent's waist as tightly as possible, preventing them from tightening their grip on you. Now, drop your weight and use your legs to lift your opponent off the mat. Twist your body as you drop down, creating enough space to break free from the bear hug. Once free, take advantage of your opponent's vulnerability to regain control of the match.

Waist Lock Escapes

A waist lock can be difficult to escape, but it isn't impossible. You can use the "Granby Roll" technique to free yourself. Tuck your head and roll your body to the side of the waist lock. As you do, grab your opponent's ankles, and pull them toward you. It opens their grip on your waist, allowing you to move away and regain control. Once free, use your techniques to take charge of the match.

Being caught in a top position can be daunting, but with these effective wrestling escapes, it is easy to regain control of the match. Mastering these top-position escapes takes practice, but they can become second nature with hard work and dedication. Knowing how to escape your opponent's grips can turn the tide of a wrestling bout in your favor. With these top-position escapes in your arsenal, you'll be well-equipped to handle even the most formidable opponents.

Bottom Position Escapes

Wrestling is a challenging and physical sport demanding high-level skills to dominate an opponent. It combines technique, strength, and endurance, requiring constant training. The bottom position is one of the most challenging positions in wrestling and is difficult to escape from. This section discusses effective bottom-position escapes wrestlers can use to escape from this position.

Granby Roll Escape

Granby rolls can be effective when escaping from the bottom position.

The Granby Roll is one of the most common bottom position escapes in wrestling. It requires speed, flexibility, and coordination. The Granby Roll starts when the wrestler on the bottom position initiates a roll while keeping their opponent's weight off them. Wrestlers should use their hands to keep the weight off as they bridge and roll in the opposite direction. Once the roll is complete, the wrestler must create distance from their opponent. The Granby Roll is an effective escape helping wrestlers transition from the bottom to a neutral position.

Switching Bases Escape

Wrestlers can use the Switching Bases Escape as another effective bottom position escape from their opponent's control. The wrestler creates space between themselves and their opponent. The wrestler in the bottom position should use their lower body to push their opponent's arms to create an opening. Once the wrestler creates this space, they must use their arms to switch their base and get back on their feet. This escape is effective because it allows the wrestler in the bottom position to get out from under their opponent more quickly.

Hip Heists Escape

The Hip Heist is another practical bottom-position escape wrestlers use to escape their opponent's control. The wrestler uses their hips to create space between themselves and their opponent. The wrestler in the bottom position posts their hands on the mat, lifting their hips. Next, the wrestler should shift their weight to one side while kicking their opposite leg backward to create space to escape. The Hip Heist is an effective escape helping wrestlers quickly move from the bottom to a neutral position.

Leg Laces Escape

The Leg Lace is another bottom position escape wrestlers can use to escape their opponent's control. The wrestler creates space between themself and their opponent by lacing or tying their legs together. The wrestler on the bottom puts their hands on the mat and laces their legs together. The wrestler lifts their hips to create space between them and their opponent. Once the wrestler has created the space, they use their arms to switch their base and get back on their feet. The Leg Lace is another effective escape helping wrestlers quickly move from the bottom to a neutral position.

Bridge Escape

The Bridge is the final bottom position escape wrestlers can use to escape their opponent's control. The wrestler creates space between themselves and their opponent by bridging in the opposite direction. The wrestler posts their hands on the mat, arching their back to lift their hips. The wrestler then uses their hands and feet to bridge away from their opponent. Once the wrestler has created the space, they use their arms to switch their base and get back on their feet. The Bridge is just one more effective escape helping wrestlers quickly move from the bottom to a neutral position.

The bottom position is challenging to escape from, requiring skills and training to escape. The Granby Roll, Switching Bases, and Hip Heists are three effective bottom position escapes wrestlers can use to transition from the bottom to a neutral position. These moves require speed, flexibility, and coordination. However, they help wrestlers escape their opponent's control and return to their feet. These escapes take time and practice to perfect, but they are practical tools for wrestlers to win a match once mastered.

Defense Techniques

Wrestling is a sport requiring offensive and defensive skills. While many wrestlers are great at attacking their opponents, wrestling is equally about defending against the opponent's attack. This section discusses defense techniques commonly used in wrestling. These techniques include the Turtle Defense, the Reverse Motion Breakdown, and the Whizzer Counter. Understanding and mastering these techniques are crucial for any wrestler wanting to excel in the sport.

Turtle Defense

The turtle defense makes it difficult for opponents to attack.

The Turtle Defense is a defensive technique wrestlers use when their opponent is about to attack them with a takedown. To execute this technique, the wrestler drops to their knees, placing their hands on the mat, forming a turtle-like position. This position makes it difficult for the opponent to attack with a takedown, as the wrestler is low to the ground, and their head is protected. The Turtle Defense is a simple yet effective technique that could save a wrestler from being taken down by their opponent.

Reverse Motion Breakdown

The reverse motion breakdown prevents opponents from gaining points.

The Reverse Motion Breakdown is a defense technique used by wrestlers when their opponent controls them on the ground. When the wrestler feels their opponent has secured control, they use the Reverse Motion Breakdown to reverse the situation. To execute this move, the wrestler quickly rolls over onto their stomach and back onto their back, taking their opponent with them. It allows the wrestler to return to the neutral position and prevent their opponent from scoring points.

Whizzer Counter

The Whizzer Counter is a defense technique wrestlers use when their opponent is attempting a single-leg takedown. To execute the Whizzer Counter, the wrestler uses their arm to push their opponent's head down, simultaneously using their opposite arm to wrap around their opponent's body and grab the elbow. This move allows the wrestler to break away from their opponent's grip and gain control of the situation. The Whizzer Counter is an effective technique to defend against a single-leg takedown.

It is essential to have excellent defense skills to become a successful wrestler. The Turtle Defense, Reverse Motion Breakdown, and Whizzer Counter are a few techniques to defend against an opponent's attack. By mastering these techniques and adding them to your arsenal, you significantly increase your chances of protecting against attacks and scoring points. Remember, wrestling necessitates offensive and defensive skills, and a well-rounded wrestler excels in both areas.

How to Increase Escaping Efficiency

Wrestling is a challenging and intense sport, full of grueling physical demands and mental challenges. One of the most crucial skills in wrestling is escaping, the ability to get out from underneath your opponent or avoid being pinned. Developing your escape skills can be the difference between winning and losing a match. This section explores the three main areas to increase your escaping efficiency in wrestling: drilling and repetition, proper body mechanics, and recognizing escape opportunities.

Drilling and Repetition

Focusing on drilling and repetition is the first key to improving your escaping efficiency in wrestling. Escaping is a skill that must be learned and practiced. Coaches should have the wrestlers work on escaping in every practice, using various techniques and scenarios. Wrestlers should also practice independently, taking time to drill specific techniques until they become second nature. The more you practice a particular escaping technique, the more comfortable and confident you become in using it during a match.

Proper Body Mechanics

Focusing on proper body mechanics is the second key to improving your escaping efficiency. Escaping is a complex movement using your whole body. You must use your hips, knees, and shoulders in a coordinated effort to maneuver your body and escape from your opponent. In addition, you must develop a strong core and leg strength to make escaping easier and more efficient. Proper body mechanics include maintaining good posture and balance to help you avoid getting stuck and unable to move.

Recognizing Escape Opportunities

The third key to improving your escaping efficiency is recognizing escape opportunities. Every match differs, so you must identify the right moment to move. It requires wrestling intelligence, reading your opponent, and anticipating their next move. It would be best to focus on developing a set of go-to escape moves while being flexible enough to adapt to your opponent's style. Be patient and keep alert for the right moment to make your move.

In addition to focusing on these three areas, here are a few other tips to improve your escaping efficiency. First, you must maintain your fitness level to stay strong and agile throughout the match. Practicing visualization techniques to help you mentally prepare for escaping scenarios would be best. Finally, don't let your ego get in the way of improving your escape skills. You must be willing to learn new techniques from coaches, teammates, and opponents.

Escaping is a fundamental skill in wrestling, and improving your efficiency in escaping can make all the difference. So, you must focus on drilling and repetition, proper body mechanics, and recognizing escape opportunities. By practicing these three areas and incorporating additional tips, you will become a better wrestler and a more successful competitor. Remember, every match offers a new challenge, and by improving your escape skills, you will be better equipped to face whatever comes your way.

Chapter 8: Pinning Combinations

Wrestling is an art form where strength, technique, and strategy converge to create pinning combinations. As a wrestler, you must clearly understand how to take your opponent down, control them, and ultimately pin them to the mat. It takes practice, discipline, and a fearless attitude to master the art of wrestling, especially with pinning combinations. But once you've learned it, there's nothing more exhilarating than feeling your opponent give in and surrender to your skillful pin.

Wrestling pin combinations will help you become a better wrestler.
https://commons.wikimedia.org/wiki/File:DF-SD-01-06921.jpg

So, let's grab our wrestling gear, hit the mat, and perfect pinning combinations until they come as naturally as breathing. This chapter explains the fundamentals of combining moves to become a proficient wrestler and how to create effective pinning combinations. It covers movements to optimize combinations, strategies to make them effective, beginner combos to practice, and advanced techniques.

Movements to Optimize Combinations

One of the keys to success in wrestling is combining various moves to take down your opponent seamlessly and effectively. Combining various techniques allows wrestlers to gain the upper hand in a match and ultimately emerge victorious. This section explores movements to help wrestlers optimize their combinations, increasing their chances of competition success. It examines combining strikes, locks, and holds and flowing between moves.

Combining Strikes

Strikes are essential components of wrestling to take down your opponent effectively. When combined creatively, they can be a powerful weapon in your arsenal. The key to effectively combining strikes is always to think of your next move. For instance, you can throw an elbow strike, then seamlessly transition into a double-leg takedown to take your opponent down. Another effective technique is combining a straight punch with a leg sweep. This involves throwing a punch, then quickly stepping behind your opponent and sweeping their leg. This move catches them off guard and helps imbalance them enough to take them down.

Combining Locks and Holds

Locks and holds are some of the most influential wrestling techniques. Combined, they can be even more powerful. To combine locks and holds, grip your opponent's wrist, giving you control over their arm. Then, use this hold to lock their arm and simultaneously get behind them, putting you in a highly advantageous position where you can easily take them down. Another effective combination is using a half-nelson to set up a cradle. This technique involves locking up your opponent's arm with a half-nelson, then rolling them onto their back with a cradle. This move requires a lot of practice and skill, but it can be a game-changer in a match.

Flowing between Moves

Finally, one of the most crucial aspects of combining movements in wrestling is flowing between them seamlessly. You must anticipate your opponent's next move and quickly adjust your strategy. For example, suppose you're going for a takedown, and your opponent counters. In that case, you immediately transition into a different move to maintain control. Another critical factor is combining moves complementing each other. For example, you can set up a double-leg takedown with a jab-cross combination. The jab-cross will distract your opponent and create an opening for you to go for the takedown.

Strategies for Effective Combinations

Wrestling is a dynamic and highly technical sport requiring great skill, strength, and endurance. Whether you're a beginner or an experienced wrestler, mastering combination moves is essential to take your game to the next level. You can develop effective combinations in various ways, but it all boils down to three crucial strategies: identifying weaknesses and strengths, capitalizing on your opponent's weaknesses, and developing adaptability. This section delves deeper into these three strategies and provides practical tips to boost your performance to become a more formidable wrestler.

Identifying Weaknesses and Strengths

The first step toward developing effective combinations is identifying your strengths and weaknesses as a wrestler. Analyzing your matches helps you identify areas where you excel and areas for improvement. This knowledge is crucial as it enables you to build on your strengths and overcome weaknesses. Once you know your strengths and weaknesses, you can tailor your training to address these areas. For instance, if you're stronger on your feet than on the mat, you should focus more on your ground game. Similarly, if you lack endurance, work on cardio exercises and drills to build stamina.

Using the Opponent's Weaknesses

The next strategy is focusing on your opponent's weaknesses. As you gain experience, you learn that every wrestler has specific weaknesses which can be exploited. Recognizing these weaknesses, whether a lack of endurance, poor balance, or a susceptibility to certain moves, puts you at a significant advantage. One way to develop this skill is by watching matches and analyzing your opponent's wrestling style. Look at their past performances and see if they struggled in any areas. Then, use this knowledge to develop moves and combinations to effectively exploit these weaknesses and put your opponent on the defensive.

Developing Adaptability

Finally, adaptability is one of the most crucial aspects of developing effective combinations. Wrestling is an unpredictable sport, and you must think on your feet and adjust your strategy as the match progresses. Developing adaptability means assessing the situation and quickly altering your game plan accordingly. One way to build adaptability is to practice and refine your moves constantly. Then, as you get more comfortable with the techniques, experiment with different variations and create new combinations. This method will help you prepare for unexpected situations and give you more tools to work with during a match.

Beginner Combos to Practice

Winning a wrestling match is about being stronger than your opponent and using the proper techniques at the right time. One way to improve your technique is to practice beginner combos. Combos are a series of moves combined to gain an advantage over your opponent. This section discusses some basic combos that beginners should practice to improve their wrestling skills.

Basic Striking Combos

Basic striking combos are essential in wrestling. They use strikes to create openings in your opponent's defense, then capitalize on them with takedowns or throws. Some basic striking combos include the jab-cross, jab-uppercut, and the overhand-right.

- The jab-cross is a standard combo to create distance from your opponent and strike. The jab is a quick, powerful punch aimed at the opponent's face or body. The cross is a straight punch aimed at the opponent's chin or chest. This combo can be used to set up a takedown or a throw.
- The jab-uppercut combo is another basic combo to create openings for takedowns or throws. The jab keeps the opponent at a distance, while the uppercut closes the distance and strikes. The uppercut is a punch aimed at the opponent's chin or body. This combo works best when you get the opponent against the cage or in the corner of the mat.

- The overhand-right combo is a powerful combo to strike with force. The overhand-right is a wide, looping punch aimed at the opponent's chin or cheek. This combo is best used when your opponent is not expecting it and must react quickly. The overhand right can set up a takedown or throw.

Essential Locks and Holds Combos

Locks and holds combos are another vital aspect of wrestling. They use leverage and pressure to control your opponent's body, immobilizing them. Some essential locks and holds combos include the armbar, the kimura, and the rear-naked choke.

- The arm bar is an effective lock to control the opponent's arm. This lock involves grabbing the opponent's arm and wrapping your legs around it. Then, you apply pressure to the opponent's elbow, forcing them to submit or risk a broken arm. You can use this lock when on top of your opponent or at the bottom.
- The kimura is another effective lock to control the opponent's arm. This lock involves grabbing your opponent's wrist and twisting it behind their back. Then, use your other hand to apply pressure to their elbow, forcing them to submit or risk injury. Again, the kimura can be used from the top or bottom position.
- The rear-naked choke is a well-known submission hold controlling the opponent's neck. This hold involves wrapping your arms around the opponent's neck and squeezing until they submit or pass out. This hold is best used when you have the opponent's back.

Beginner Flows

Beginner flows are a combination of striking and grappling techniques flowing from one to the other. These flows help build muscle memory and improve reaction time. Some beginner flows include:

- The jab-takedown flow uses the jab to create an opening for a takedown. For example, you jab the opponent's face, create distance, and shoot for a takedown.
- The jab-cross-shoot flow is a combination of striking and takedown techniques. Start with a jab, throw a cross, and then shoot in for a takedown.

- The double jab-double leg takedown flow combines striking and takedown techniques. Start with two jabs, create distance, and shoot for a double-leg takedown.

Effective Combinations

In wrestling, one of the most critical aspects of the sport is combining moves seamlessly. When done correctly, combining different moves can catch your opponent off guard, putting them on the defensive and ultimately leading to a victory. This section delves into some of the most effective combinations in wrestling.

The Multi-Strike Combination

The Multi-Strike combination is a powerful tool in a wrestler's arsenal. It combines different strikes to create an opening for a takedown or pin. This combination can include punches, kicks, or even headbutts – for instance, some wrestlers like to lead with a punch to the stomach, followed by a kick to the leg or a headbutt to the chest. The idea is to keep your opponent guessing and off-balance, leaving them open to your takedown attempt. When executed correctly, the multi-strike combination can be devastating.

The Lock and Strike Combination

The Lock and Strike combination is another effective way to take down your opponent. This technique involves locking up with your opponent and striking them with a series of blows to create an opening for a takedown or submission hold. This combination includes strikes to the head, gut, or legs. Once your opponent is stunned by the strikes, use the lock to leverage them into a vulnerable position. Many wrestlers use this combination to set up a chokehold or armbar.

The Evasive Combination

The Evasive combination is all about movement. This combination uses quick, evasive movements to avoid your opponent's strikes while setting up your takedown attempt. One typical evasive move is the "slip-and-rip." You slip to the side of your opponent's punch, then strike with a short hook or uppercut. Another standard evasive move is the "duck-under." You duck under your opponent's arm, then go for the takedown. The Evasive combination is excellent for wrestlers who are good at reading their opponent's movements and can react quickly.

Mastering pinning combinations in wrestling is critical in taking down your opponent. By practicing these combinations during training, you will become a formidable opponent on the mat and dominate your opponent in the ring. Remember, wrestling is all about technique and knowing how to use each move to your advantage. So, practice your combinations, learn to read your opponent's movements and reactions, and become the champion wrestler you were born to be.

Advanced Techniques

Wrestling, known for its unique blend of strength, agility, and technique, has evolved into a competitive sport demanding physical and mental skills. As a wrestler, developing advanced techniques is essential for staying ahead of the competition. This section discusses advanced techniques to help you dominate on the mat.

Advanced Combinations for One-on-One Combat

One of the most crucial aspects of wrestling is stringing together different techniques to create a compelling combination. Advanced wrestlers know how to combine various grips, throws, and takedowns fluidly. To elevate your game, you must have a solid understanding of the fundamentals and build on them. For example, a basic shoulder throw can be combined with a leg sweep for a decisive takedown. As you progress, mix up different techniques to surprise your opponent, like a fake shot followed by a single-leg takedown. You can outsmart and outmaneuver your opponent on the mat by mastering advanced combinations.

Grandmaster Combinations for Multiple Opponents

One of the most common challenges a wrestler faces is overcoming multiple opponents simultaneously. Grandmasters have developed techniques to help overcome this challenge. One approach is using the momentum of one opponent against the other. For example, you can use an arm drag on one wrestler to throw them into the path of another. Using peripheral vision and situational awareness is crucial when taking on multiple opponents. Another advanced technique is using a double-leg takedown on one wrestler, then using the momentum to roll into submission on the other. These advanced combinations require precision, timing, and agility but can be game-changers in a tough match.

Combining Strategies and Mental Triggers

Wrestling isn't only about physical techniques. It's also about being innovative and strategic. Elite wrestlers understand how to execute moves and when to use them. Mental triggers give you a significant advantage, like understanding your opponent's weaknesses or capitalizing on their mistakes. Combining different strategies can help keep your opponent off-balance. For example, if you're known for your strong takedown abilities, start with a stand-up the next time, catching your opponent off-guard. You can become a formidable opponent by incorporating mental strategies with technical ones.

Using Feints and Fakes

Feints and fakes can be powerful tools in wrestling. A fake or feint can be as simple as pretending to shoot for a leg takedown to cause the opponent to reach down for a defense opening their arms to counter and throw. Feints can test your opponent's reactions before going in for the actual move. You can create openings in your opponent's defense and put them off balance using feints and fakes.

Advanced wrestling techniques take time and practice to perfect. However, combining different styles, utilizing strategic mental triggers, and incorporating feints and fakes can make it easier to dominate your opponents on the mat. By mastering these techniques, you can anticipate your opponent's moves, create openings, and execute decisive takedowns and throws. Remember, only some strategies or plans will lead to success. Instead, it would be best to experiment with different combinations to find what works best. Then, keep honing your skills and refining your techniques, and you'll be well on your way to becoming an elite wrestler.

Chapter 9: Training at Home

Are you tired of missing out on your wrestling training due to gym closures or scheduling conflicts? Don't let that stop you from achieving your goals. With the right equipment, you can efficiently train at home and maintain strength, technique, and endurance. Whether setting up a mat in your garage, investing in a wrestling dummy, or simply finding creative ways to substitute a partner, there are endless possibilities to keep your training on track.

With dedication and a focused mindset, you can turn your home into a formidable training arena and stay ahead of the competition. This chapter outlines the drills and exercises you can practice alone at home, with and without equipment. Training alone and practicing daily is as important as practicing with an opponent and improving skills and physical condition.

Solo Drills

Wrestlers must be sharp and precise with their techniques, which comes with constant practice. Sometimes, injury or lack of partners or facilities necessitate solo training. Solo drills are essential in helping wrestlers refine and develop their skills while training independently. This section explores some solo drills wrestlers can undertake to improve.

Shadowboxing

Shadowboxing helps with reenacting wrestling techniques.
https://www.pexels.com/photo/man-in-black-t-shirt-and-black-shorts-standing-on-brown-wooden-floor-4753985/

Shadowboxing is one of the most fundamental solo drills for wrestlers. The technique requires visualization and reenactment of wrestling techniques in the air. It is helpful in refining movements and techniques, mastering balance and coordination, and developing footwork and range. Shadowboxing solo drills are completed devoid of equipment or props. Moreover, the drive behind shadowboxing is to simulate an actual match, and wrestlers must execute their techniques with precision and power, like in actual competition. Wrestlers must focus on their footwork, head movement, stance, and hand positioning when shadowboxing.

Footwork and Movement Drills

Wrestlers need excellent footwork to outpace their opponents, control their range, and maintain balance while executing a technique. Movement drills are essential in developing the flexibility and agility required for wrestling. The exercises help shift weight swiftly from one foot to the other, pivot, and maintain variances in the opponent's movement. Footwork and movement drills include pivoting, shuffling, side-step, jump rope, and more.

Pad Work Drills

Pad work drills are instrumental in developing proper weight distribution, range, and striking techniques. The pads offer resistance and replicate an opponent's body, helping wrestlers develop precision and power in their targeting. One of the most popular pad work drills is the focus mitt drill. Wrestlers focus on attaining a rhythm and flow in their striking techniques to simulate an opponent's movement.

Heavy Bag Drills

Heavy bag drills are essential in building strength, endurance, and explosiveness in wrestlers. In addition, the drills are instrumental in refining targeting and movements in real-life situations. Heavy bag drills involve striking a heavy bag with intensity and precision. Performers use a range of strikes, such as kicks, punches, and knees, to work on form, power, and range. Wrestlers must focus on maintaining proper technique in their strikes, ensuring the safety of their joints.

Partner Drills and Exercises

While solo practice sessions are crucial for personal growth, partner drills and exercises are essential for perfecting wrestling techniques and building problem-solving skills. In addition, they help wrestlers practice specific techniques, improve their timing and awareness, and build endurance to enhance their competitive edge. This section discusses some of the most effective partner drills and exercises for wrestlers. Whether new to wrestling or an experienced grappler, these exercises and drills will help you sharpen your skills and become a formidable opponent.

Sparring

Sparring is a staple in wrestling and is considered one of the best partner drills for grapplers. It lets you apply techniques you learned in practice to a live, competitive situation. With a partner, you can take turns attacking and defending, using all the different methods, like shooting and sprawling. Sparring sessions can be conducted in various formats, but free sparring and live wrestling are two of the most popular. Free sparring allows wrestlers to practice their moves and counters without predetermined actions. In contrast, live wrestling limits the techniques used in the match to give wrestlers the feeling of a more organized wrestling practice.

Partner Pad Work Drills

Partner pad work drills are excellent for practicing and improving the power and accuracy of your strikes and throws. These drills involve working with a partner who holds pads, giving you targets to hit. For instance, the focus mitt drill involves striking moving targets (mitts) held by your partner. This drill allows you to work on your punches, kicks, and other striking techniques while increasing your power and speed. The partner can hold pads and give you targets to throw at to help perfect your throws and takedowns.

Clinching and Grappling Exercises

Clinching and grappling exercises improve positioning, control, and submission techniques. They develop a firm grip and arm strength. Drills like pummeling, where wrestlers clinch and reposition their arms while in a stand-up position, or drilling various takedowns and defenses are some of the best drills for demonstrating these skills. Another exercise to increase your grip strength is the monkey grip drill. This drill is holding a partner's wrist and hand while they pull their arm away. The goal is to secure your grip and maintain a steady stance while your partner attempts to break free.

Conditioning Drills

Although wrestling matches typically last only a few minutes, they require high endurance and stamina. Therefore, conditioning drills are best for wrestlers to build endurance and improve fitness. One drill is the "Suicide Drill." The drill involves running at full speed from one line to another, followed by a reversal of direction to complete the next run. The drill is performed in a "ladder" format, where the distance you run is increased with each repetition. Another effective drill for conditioning is the bear crawl. In this drill, you get on all fours and crawl forward by moving your left hand and right foot simultaneously, then your other hand and foot. The aim is to crawl a specific number of meters or until you're too tired to continue.

Reaction Drills

Reaction drills are essential in all combat sports, especially wrestling. They improve wrestlers' ability to anticipate their opponent's next move while developing punch and response timing. One of the most popular reaction drills in wrestling is the shadow drill. This drill is shadow wrestling with a partner, where they execute a series of moves, and the other wrestler responds with countermoves to improve reflexes and reaction time. This drill also improves footwork, head movement, and overall body control.

At-Home Exercises without Equipment

Wrestling is a sport requiring physical and mental agility and strength. It is entertaining and helps improve an individual's overall health. If you're a wrestler, you know how important it is to maintain body strength. The good news is you can easily do this at home without gym equipment. Here are some at-home wrestling exercises to do without equipment.

Jump Rope

Jumping rope might seem like a simple activity, but it's one of the best exercises to improve agility, coordination, and footwork. It is an effective cardio exercise improving cardiovascular fitness and endurance. Jumping rope consistently for at least 10 minutes can burn up to 100 calories. As a wrestler, jumping rope improves balance and quick footwork, which are essential for taking down your opponent.

Burpees

Burpees are a full-body workout engaging every muscle group. It is a high-intensity interval training (HIIT) improving cardiovascular fitness while building muscles. Burpees are easy-to-do workouts requiring no equipment and can be modified according to your fitness level. It is also an excellent exercise to improve endurance and stamina.

Push-Ups and Sit-Ups

Push-ups and sit-ups are two classic exercises that can be done anywhere. They are affordable and require no equipment. They are essential exercises for wrestlers as they help develop upper body strength, core stability, and balance. Push-ups work on your chest, shoulders, triceps, and upper back, while sit-ups improve abdominal muscles.

Squats and Lunges

Squats and lunges are two critical exercises to build leg muscles. They help improve your balance, flexibility, and mobility. Squats work on your quads, hamstrings, and glutes, while lunges work on your calves, quads, and glutes. Regularly doing squats and lunges can improve agility, endurance, and balance, which are essential for wrestling.

Running, Cycling, or Swimming

Cardiovascular exercise is essential for any fitness routine. Running, cycling, or swimming can improve cardiovascular health while keeping you in excellent physical shape. Running helps burn calories, increases endurance, and builds leg muscles. Cycling is a low-impact exercise that builds quad and hamstring muscles while increasing stamina. Swimming is an excellent low-impact exercise engaging your entire body while improving cardiovascular health.

At-Home Exercises with Equipment

Wrestling is one of the most challenging sports, requiring strength, stamina, and agility. But if you're a wrestling enthusiast, you don't need to hit the gym to maintain a good physique. Instead, you can do it right from the comfort of your home. Here are some of the best at-home wrestling exercises with equipment to help you get in shape, stay healthy, and improve your wrestling game.

Resistance Bands

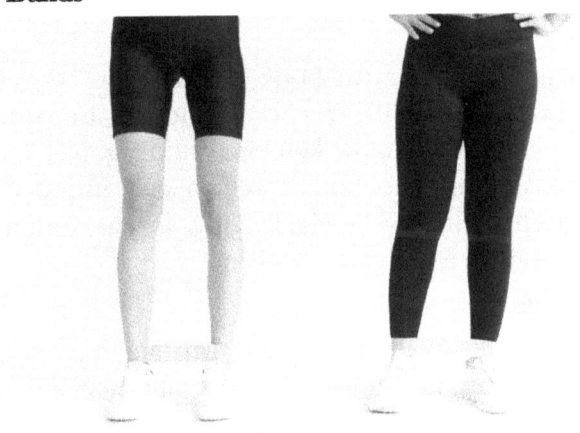

Resistance bands can improve strength and tone the body.
https://www.pexels.com/photo/people-workout-using-resistance-bands-6516206/

Resistance bands are a great way to improve your strength and tone your body. Wrap the bands around your feet, hold them in your hands, and perform exercises like the standing chest press, bicep curls, tricep extensions, and standing rows. You can use the bands to work on your legs by doing squats, lunges, and leg curls. In addition, you can adjust the intensity of the exercises by using different bands with varying resistance levels, making it an excellent workout for beginners and seasoned wrestlers.

Medicine Balls

Medicine balls are another piece of equipment to help you get into shape. They come in various weights and sizes, so choose a comfortable and suitable one. Hold the ball with both hands and perform exercises like the overhead press, chest pass, side throws, and slams. You can do partner exercises like the Russian twist, wall pass, and sit-ups. These exercises are great for developing core strength, speed, and agility.

Punching Bag or Punch Mitts

Punching is an essential component of wrestling, and a punching bag or punch mitts can be a great way to improve technique and endurance. Hang the bag in your garage, or buy a pair of punch mitts and have a partner hold them up for you. Then, practice your jabs, hooks, crosses, and uppercuts for a great cardio workout and help you tone your arms and upper body.

Kettlebells

Kettlebells are great for full-body workouts with excellent results. They come in various weights, so choose one you are comfortable with. Then, perform exercises like the kettlebell swing, goblet squat, clean and jerk, and Turkish get-up to build strength and improve your overall conditioning. Kettlebells can be challenging, so start with a lower weight and work your way up as you get stronger.

Ankle Weights

Ankle weights help you develop strength and power in your lower body. Wear them during exercises like leg lifts, calf raises, and side leg lifts. Wear them while walking or jogging for a great workout for building endurance. However, be careful not to overdo it, as ankle weights can place too much stress on your joints and lead to injury.

Tips for Training Alone at Home

The current health crisis has presented new challenges for wrestlers who are used to training in a team environment. However, you can continue your passion for the sport. With some creativity, you can continue to improve your skills and stay in shape while training alone at home. Here are some tips on preparing yourself, remaining focused and motivated, and tracking your progress.

Set a Schedule

Maintaining a regular schedule is one of the most important aspects of training alone. Without a coach or teammates, losing focus and becoming less committed to your training sessions is easy. Avoid this by setting a specific time each day for your workout and sticking to it rigorously. Create a schedule that works best for you and allows you to focus on your daily activities.

Choose a Variety of Exercises

Choosing a variety of exercises to improve different aspects of your wrestling game is crucial to developing a well-rounded training program. Start by selecting basic exercises developing strength, speed, and endurance, like push-ups, squats, and sit-ups. Next, add plyometric exercises like box jumps, bound jumps, and jump squats. For power development and bodyweight exercises, include crab walks, burpees, and planks.

Focus on Technique and Form

Wrestling requires exceptional technique and form. To reach your full potential, you must take time to work on your form and ensure your techniques are performed correctly. Although analyzing yourself during training is challenging, you can make significant improvements by watching tutorial videos and carefully breaking down the movements.

Don't Neglect Conditioning

In wrestling, conditioning is everything. It determines whether or not you'll last an entire match and help you win. When training by yourself, it's essential to include conditioning exercises that mimic the intensity and duration of a wrestling match. Activities like running, sprints, hill climbs, and interval training will build a strong foundation.

Track Your Progress

While training alone, tracking your progress is vital to stay motivated and to help you to document your gains. Keep a journal or download a training app to help you gauge your progress and monitor areas for improvement. Knowing your achievements helps you turn challenging training sessions into more positive experiences and pushes you closer to your goals.

Wrestling can be challenging but also the most rewarding. With discipline and dedication, you can improve your skills, continue to train alone, and take your wrestling game to the next level. Setting a schedule, choosing a variety of exercises, focusing on technique and form, not neglecting to condition, tracking your progress, staying motivated, and taking regular breaks encourage progress and keep you inspired through this challenging time. Don't be convinced that training without equipment or alone is inadequate. It could make or break your wrestling career.

Chapter 10: Training and Coaching Youth

Wrestling isn't just a sport. It's a way of life. Teaching youth the art of wrestling takes dedication, patience, and the right coaching strategies. It's not enough to show them the techniques and moves; discipline, resilience, and self-confidence that come with being a wrestler must be instilled in them. As a coach, it's crucial to understand the different learning styles of each wrestler and provide a supportive environment encouraging their strengths and weaknesses.

By investing in developing young wrestlers, you're building outstanding athletes and honorable leaders who will carry the lessons they learned on the mat into every aspect of their lives. This chapter aims to provide coaches and parents with the necessary information to ensure each wrestler is safe, nurtured, and equipped with a fun learning environment to thrive. Remember, with the proper guidance and support, these budding wrestlers will reach their full potential.

Safety and Precautions for Young Wrestlers

Young wrestlers should use protective gear.
https://unsplash.com/photos/DCqXIFXoqr0?utm_source=unsplash&utm_medium=referral&utm_content=creditShareLink

Wrestling is a challenging and physically demanding sport. While it might look like a fun game for many kids to play with friends, it is essential to remember that wrestlers are at a heightened risk for injury. As a parent or coach, ensuring wrestlers practice this sport safely, in and outside the ring, is crucial. This section outlines some essential safety precautions for young wrestlers every coach, parent, or athlete should know.

Protective Equipment for Wrestlers

Many young wrestlers jump into the sport without the right protective gear. However, proper gear is essential to keep the wrestlers safe while participating in the sport. The following are crucial protective equipment every young wrestler must have:

- **Headgear:** Headgear is the most crucial protective gear a wrestler can wear. It minimizes and avoids critical head and ear injuries.
- **Wrestling Shoes:** Wrestling shoes protect wrestlers' feet and provide grip on the mat.

- **Mouthguard:** A mouthguard is recommended to protect the teeth and jaws from injuries. A flying headbutt, or an accidental elbow to the mouth, could easily knock a tooth out or cause severe jaw and neck injuries.
- **Knee Pads:** Knee pads are not necessary but highly recommended to protect the knees and prevent scrapes, cuts, or bruises.

Additional Rules for Safety and Fun

Wrestling is not just about physical strength. It's about following rules and techniques. Here are some additional rules and tips to ensure the safety and fun of every young wrestler:

- Always respect the opponent and avoid rough or unsportsmanlike conduct when practicing or competing.
- Avoid mimicking professional techniques seen on TV, as they can be dangerous for young wrestlers.
- Follow weight requirements to avoid competing with someone much larger or heavier than you.
- Hydration is critical. Wrestlers should drink plenty of water and avoid sugary drinks before, during, and after matches.

Learning the Basics of Wrestling

Before young wrestlers take to the ring and compete, they must learn the basics of wrestling. Proper techniques and rules can help prevent injuries. Professional coaches should handle teaching these fundamental techniques. Here are some essential strategies for beginners:

- **Takedowns:** Teach children proper shooting techniques to avoid head and neck injuries.
- **Escape:** This technique can help wrestlers get back on their feet or avoid being pinned.
- **Pinning Combination:** This technique can help wrestlers to dominate in a match and get their opponent onto the mat.

The Importance of Rest and Recovery

Rest is essential for young wrestlers to recover from the physical and mental stress of the sport. Young wrestlers should not be pushed too hard in training, as it can lead to burnout and injuries. Proper rest and recovery help avoid muscle strains and other injuries.

Promoting Respect for the Sport

Teaching young wrestlers the importance of respecting the sport and their opponents is crucial. As a coach or parent, it's your responsibility to ensure your wrestlers understand the importance of respecting the sport and demonstrating good behavior. This section discusses ways to promote respect for the sport in young wrestlers and how to lay the foundation for positive behavior.

Being a Good Coach or Parent

As a coach or parent, it's essential to lead by example. Young wrestlers look up to those around them and mirror their behavior. If you exhibit positive behavior and respect the sport and opponents, you're more likely to inspire the same behavior in your wrestlers. Clarify your expectations and demonstrate them consistently.

Maintaining open communication with your wrestlers is crucial. Encourage them to express their thoughts, concerns, and ideas. By doing so, you let them know their opinions matter, and they can learn from constructive criticism. Ensure you are approachable and supportive, understand what motivates your wrestlers, and provide the necessary support.

Teaching Good Behavior

Wrestlers should be taught the sport's rules and the code of conduct early. Emphasize the values of integrity, humility, and respect for opponents, on and off the mat. They must know they represent themselves and their team, school, and community. Encourage them to strive toward excellence and remind them of the importance of respecting everyone. Inculcate this behavior by rewarding those who show positive behavior.

Teaching them good sportsmanship is another behavioral aspect essential in wrestling and life. Congratulating your opponent, helping them back up, and never gloating are qualities of good sportsmanship. This behavior should be regularly reinforced since it promotes respect toward everyone.

Rewards for Good Conduct

One way to promote respectful behavior is to incentivize positive behavior. Rewarding wrestlers for good behavior promotes a positive environment and helps reinforce the values of respect and integrity. For example, reward them with tokens, badges, certificates, or anything the wrestler finds valuable. This motivation will include better behavior, and others will emulate their behavior to receive recognition.

Wrestling is an individual sport, but it takes a team to be successful. Therefore, create a team atmosphere that instills unity, respect, and mutual support. As everyone feels more united and valued, it could bring a new level of fulfillment and satisfaction to your wrestling journey.

Giving the Kids a Chance to Shine

Wrestling is about physical strength, mental toughness, and strategic thinking. For young wrestlers, it can be a challenging but rewarding experience. For parents and coaches, it can be a chance to mold future champions and instill essential life skills. This section explores how encouraging and supporting participation, creating, and achieving goals, celebrating success, and learning from mistakes can help young wrestlers shine.

Encouraging and Supporting Participation

One of the most important things parents and coaches can do for young wrestlers is to encourage and support their participation. It means attending their matches and providing emotional support, positive feedback, and constructive criticism. Encouragement comes in many forms, such as offering encouragement before a game, praising hard work and improvement, and recognizing a wrestler's achievements. In addition, supporting participation includes ensuring young wrestlers have access to appropriate gear, transportation to matches, and access to coaches and other resources. Finally, parents and coaches can help young wrestlers stay motivated and enjoy the sport by fostering a supportive environment.

Creating Goals and Achieving Them

Setting goals is an essential part of any sport; wrestling is no exception. Goal-setting helps young wrestlers stay focused and motivated, measure their progress, and celebrate their successes. Goals can be short-term or long-term, including milestones like winning a match or achieving a certain fitness level. Coaches and parents can help young wrestlers create achievable goals that are realistic but challenging to help develop their skills and improve performance. By setting and achieving goals, young wrestlers gain confidence in their abilities and develop a growth mindset.

Celebrating Success and Learning from Mistakes

In wrestling, as in life, success and failure are vital learning opportunities. When young wrestlers achieve their goals or win a match, it is essential to celebrate their accomplishments and recognize their hard work and dedication. It can take many forms, such as praising their efforts, giving them rewards, or acknowledging them publicly. Celebrating success helps young wrestlers feel valued and appreciated and motivates them to continue working hard. At the same time, learning from mistakes and setbacks is essential. After a loss or failure, coaches and parents must help young wrestlers identify what went wrong and how they can improve. It can include constructive criticism, practicing specific skills, or finding new ways to approach a challenge.

Creating the Right Environment for Learning

Young wrestlers, especially those just starting, need a safe, positive, and encouraging environment to develop their skills effectively and grow as athletes. This section highlights some essential tips that coaches and parents can use to create the right environment for young wrestlers.

Ensuring the Environment Is Safe and Stress-Free

Safety is the first and most important factor in creating a positive learning environment. Coaches and parents must ensure the wrestling environment is safe for young athletes to practice without risking injury, including maintaining proper equipment, ensuring the wrestling mats are clean and well-maintained, and teaching athletes good techniques to avoid injuries.

Additionally, the environment must be stress-free. Young wrestlers can easily get overwhelmed and discouraged if they feel pressured to perform or fear making mistakes. Instead, coaches and parents should focus on creating an atmosphere of positivity and encouragement where athletes feel comfortable and supported and are not afraid to take risks and try new things.

Encouraging Fun While Learning

Wrestling is a challenging and demanding sport, but it doesn't mean it can't be fun. Coaches and parents should strive to make learning wrestling skills an enjoyable experience by incorporating games, challenges, and other activities to engage young athletes and keep them motivated. For example, coaches can organize wrestling drills and games, allowing wrestlers to practice their skills while having fun. Parents can also get involved by attending matches and cheering for their children, showing them that wrestling is not just about winning but also about having a good time.

Making Wrestling Instruction Enjoyable

It's essential to make wrestling instruction enjoyable and engaging so young wrestlers stay focused and motivated throughout their training. Therefore, coaches should vary their teaching methods and use different techniques to communicate new skills and techniques effectively. For example, coaches can use video demonstrations, group discussions, and one-on-one coaching sessions to teach wrestling skills. They can provide regular feedback and encouragement and create individualized training plans that cater to each athlete's strengths and weaknesses.

Fostering a Growth Mindset

Last (but not least), coaches and parents should foster a growth mindset in young wrestlers. The growth mindset is the belief that skills and abilities can be improved through hard work, dedication, and persistence. It encourages young athletes to embrace challenges and setbacks as opportunities to learn and grow and not to be discouraged by them. Parents and coaches can help develop a growth mindset by praising wrestlers for their effort and progress instead of only their results. They should encourage wrestlers to set realistic and achievable goals and celebrate their achievements.

Creating a positive and productive learning environment is essential for young wrestlers to develop their skills and grow as athletes. Coaches and parents create an environment where young athletes can thrive and reach their full potential by prioritizing safety, encouraging fun, making wrestling instruction enjoyable, and fostering a growth mindset. As coaches and parents, it's your responsibility to provide proper guidance and support and instill the love of the sport in young wrestlers to keep them engaged and motivated for years.

Considerations during Practice and Matches

Wrestling can be an excellent way for children to learn discipline, improve their physical health, and build self-confidence. However, as with any sport, wrestling requires precautions, including proper nutrition, warm-ups, and reminders of rules, which young wrestlers and parents must remember. This section provides parents and young athletes with essential considerations during practice and matches to improve safety and performance.

Proper Nutrition

While most people know nutrition is significant for an athlete, young wrestlers must have a proper diet to ensure they have the energy to compete. A sufficient and healthy diet should offer adequate carbohydrates and proteins for an athlete's growing body, sustaining the demanding training sessions and fast-paced matches. For example, a protein snack and a banana before practice or a game should provide the necessary energy to last the duration. In addition, parents can consult with coaches or nutritionists to ensure their young wrestlers get the proper nutrients.

Warm-Ups and Stretching

Wrestling demands intense physical exertion, and young wrestlers must prepare their muscles correctly before matches or practice sessions start. Therefore, coaches should lead warm-up sessions lasting up to 30 minutes. These sessions should include stretching exercises to prevent muscle injuries, agility drills to improve flexibility and explosiveness, and calisthenics like push-ups and sit-ups to improve strength. In addition, young wrestlers should be instructed on stretching correctly, including slowing down if they feel strained or pain during warm-up exercises.

Reminders for the Referee's Rules

Wrestling matches require referees to ensure all games meet the required regulations and prevent injuries like falls and injury. Therefore, young wrestlers should know the game's rules to keep matches safe and fair. For example, they should understand that grappling moves and certain grips are permitted while holds like headbutting, biting, or poking opponents' eyes are prohibited. In addition, young wrestlers must listen to their coaches and the referee's guidance and behave respectfully toward their opponents, coaches, and referees. They must be taught to deal with both mental and emotional situations, like losing a match or responding to aggressive behavior.

Stress Management

Wrestling is an intensive and challenging sport, often resulting in emotional and mental stress on young wrestlers. This stress can impact their performance during practice and matches. Educating young wrestlers about the importance of stress management techniques, such as deep breathing exercises, yoga, and visualization, helps reduce stress levels and increase their overall performance. In addition, parents can help their young wrestlers recognize their stress triggers and encourage them to practice relaxation exercises to manage their stress.

Wrestling is an exhilarating sport benefitting young athletes' physical and emotional well-being. However, young wrestlers must take the necessary precautions and follow essential considerations to remain safe and perform at their best. Proper nutrition, warm-up sessions, knowledge of the referee's rules, and stress management techniques make all the difference in young wrestlers' success on and off the mat. Therefore, parents, coaches, and young wrestlers must work together to create a safe, healthy, and successful athletic experience.

Chapter 11: Wrestling Success

Wrestling is about the dedication, hard work, and passion that goes into every practice and moment on the mat. Successful wrestlers understand that every move counts and that their mindset and preparation determine their outcome. They have the confidence and determination to face any opponent with a strategic plan and mental toughness to push through fatigue and pain. Wrestling success is earned through continuous training, sacrifice, and a "never-give-up" attitude.

The satisfaction and pride are indescribable when all the hard work pays off and you stand victorious on the mat. This chapter is dedicated to celebrating success stories of wrestlers who have achieved greatness and providing advice to help aspiring athletes achieve their dreams. These stories and tips will leave you feeling inspired and ready to take on any challenge. These wrestlers' successes are a living testament to the power of hard work and perseverance. Let's get started.

The Triumphs of Wrestling Champions

Wrestling is far more than just a sport or entertainment. It involves passion, perseverance, and dedication. Over the years, many wrestlers have crossed boundaries and achieved new milestones. Notably, some wrestlers with inspiring journeys are worth knowing. This section closely examines the success stories of wrestling champions, including John Cena, The Rock, Charlotte Flair, Hulk Hogan, and CM Punk.

John Cena

John Cena is a well-known wrestling icon.
Gage Skidmore from Peoria, AZ, United States of America, CC BY-SA 2.0 <https://creativecommons.org/licenses/by-sa/2.0>, via Wikimedia Commons: https://commons.wikimedia.org/wiki/File:John_Cena_July_2018.jpg

John Cena is a well-known wrestling icon with a vast fan base. He began his career in wrestling with the Ultimate Pro Wrestling (UPW) and then signed with the WWE in 2000. Cena has an impressive WWE record, with 25 championships to his name. His inspiring story lies in his perseverance. Cena had to work through numerous setbacks and injuries but never lost sight of his goal and worked tirelessly to get back in the game. He became one of the greatest wrestlers ever through hard work and dedication.

The Rock

The Rock, aka Dwayne Johnson, has one of the most inspiring stories in professional wrestling. He started his career in wrestling with his father, Rocky Johnson, and later joined the WWE. After years of hard work and dedication, he became one of the greatest WWE champions ever. Even after achieving great success, The Rock continued to push himself further. In addition, he pursued his passion for acting and has starred in several blockbuster movies. The Rock's tenacity and dedication to his craft make him a true inspiration.

Charlotte Flair

The daughter of wrestling legend Ric Flair, Charlotte Flair, has always had big shoes to fill. She started her wrestling career in 2012 and soon got signed with the WWE. Since then, she has won numerous titles and broken several records. Her journey to success is founded on hard work, dedication, and a passion for the sport. Flair continues to work tirelessly, inspiring women wrestlers everywhere to follow their dreams.

Hulk Hogan

Hulk Hogan is a name that echoes throughout the history of wrestling. His dynamic showmanship and in-ring presence made him one of the most recognizable faces in wrestling. Hogan started his career in Tennessee and was soon signed with the WWE. His journey to success is derived from non-stop dedication, hard work, and practice. Despite numerous setbacks, he continued to push forward and became a living legend in wrestling.

CM Punk

CM Punk began his career in wrestling with the Independent Circuit and later joined the WWE. He quickly gained popularity due to his unique personality and wrestling style. Punk became one of the most significant forces in the WWE. However, Punk felt unfulfilled despite his successes and ultimately retired in 2014. Since then, he has inspired wrestlers worldwide to pursue their dreams and push themselves further.

The stories of John Cena, The Rock, Charlotte Flair, Hulk Hogan, and CM Punk embody the fundamental traits of a true champion. Their journeys are inspiring and have set a benchmark for many wrestlers to follow in their footsteps. These wrestling icons have reached the pinnacle of their careers, not once but repeatedly. They remind us that, with hard work and strong determination, we can achieve anything we set our minds to.

Pro Tips from Pros

Pro wrestling is a physically demanding sport requiring strength, agility, and mental toughness. Becoming a pro wrestler takes a lot of hard work and dedication, but with the right approach, you can achieve your goals and take your performance to the next level. This section lists valuable professional wrestling tips to help you become a better wrestler and succeed in this exciting field.

- **Train Hard and Consistently:** The key to success in pro wrestling is to train hard and consistently. Work on your strength, agility, and endurance to become a better wrestler. Ensure you have a well-rounded workout routine, including weightlifting, cardio, and flexibility training. Regularly practicing wrestling techniques to improve your skills and build muscle memory is best.
- **Stay Positive and Believe in Yourself:** Pro wrestlers must have a positive attitude and believe in their abilities. This sport is very challenging, and there will be times when you face setbacks and failures. However, it's essential to stay positive and keep pushing forward. Believe in yourself and your abilities; never give up on your dreams.
- **Use Mentors and Coaches:** Pro wrestling is a team sport, so it's essential to have a support system, including mentors and coaches. Find a mentor who can guide you through the challenges of pro wrestling and advise you on improving your skills. Also, work with a coach who will help you develop a training program tailored to your needs.
- **Take Time to Rest and Recover:** Pro wrestling is a high-impact sport, and it's essential to rest and recover. Ensure you sleep well, eat a healthy diet, and care for your body. You must listen to your body and take breaks when needed; it will prevent injuries and ensure you consistently perform at your best.
- **Stay Focused on Your Goals:** To become a successful pro wrestler, you need clear and focused goals. Whether winning a championship, getting signed to a major wrestling organization, or simply improving your skills, ensure you have a plan and stay committed. Focus on your strengths, work on your weaknesses, and always strive to be the best wrestler you can be.

Advice for Those Pursuing Pro Wrestling

Professional wrestling is an exciting career. It's no secret that pro wrestlers are some of the most talented athletes in the world. However, to become a successful professional wrestler, every aspiring wrestler must consider certain things. This section discusses some critical advice for those pursuing pro wrestling as a career. Whether you are just starting or have been wrestling for a while, these tips will help you become a successful wrestler.

Get the Proper Training to Succeed

The first and most important piece of advice for anyone pursuing pro wrestling is to get proper training. It's not enough to be athletic or have a good physique. You must have proper training in the art of professional wrestling. Many wrestling schools and trainers exist, so take your time to research the best ones. Look for experienced trainers who have trained successful wrestlers in the past. Getting good training will help you understand the nuances of the wrestling industry and prepare you for everything that comes with it.

Find a Mentor or Coach to Guide You

In addition to getting good training, finding a mentor or coach who can help guide you is essential. It is especially important in the early stages of your career. A mentor provides valuable advice on everything from ring gear to in-ring psychology. They can introduce you to other wrestlers and promoters, which can be invaluable for making connections in the industry. Mentors can be found almost anywhere, from your wrestling school to independent shows. Take advantage of the opportunities to learn from those who have already been where you want to go.

Develop Your Mental Toughness and Stay Positive

Pro wrestling is a tricky business. The physical demands of the job are merely the beginning. You must deal with rejection, disappointment, and injuries. Therefore, you must be mentally tough and able to handle adversity to succeed in this industry. The best way is to stay positive. Focus on the things you can control, and don't get discouraged by those you can't. Instead, believe in yourself and your abilities, and keep pushing forward.

Set Realistic Goals and Stick to Them

One of the aspiring wrestlers' most significant mistakes is setting unrealistic goals. While it's important to dream big, setting achievable goals is also essential. It means setting short-term and long-term goals. For example, short-term goals include getting booked for several matches in a month. Long-term goals could be getting signed to a major wrestling promotion. Once you have set your goals, it's essential to stick to them. Stay focused and committed, and keep going even if things don't happen as quickly as you would like.

Network with Other Wrestlers and Promoters

Finally, networking is crucial to success in the pro wrestling industry. Making connections with other wrestlers and promoters in the industry is highly beneficial. Attend wrestling shows and conventions and introduce yourself to people. Offer to help at shows and events and be willing to learn from those around you. The more people you know in the industry, the better your chances of getting booked for shows and advancing your career.

Tips for Women Wrestlers

Women interested in wrestling often shy away from the sport because of the perceived physicality and the dominant presence of men. However, the sport of wrestling is equally accessible to women as it is to men. All it takes is persistence, dedication, and an unwavering belief in oneself. So, let's dive into the top tips to help women wrestlers conquer this fantastic sport.

Don't Be Afraid to Speak Up for Yourself

Women wrestlers often feel intimidated being surrounded by men. However, everyone has to go through the process of learning the sport. Speaking up and asserting your boundaries and comfort zones is essential because nobody knows you better than yourself. Do not hesitate to ask for help or guidance from your coach and teammates. Being vocal about your needs will help you gain the respect and support of others.

Start Small and Build Your Way Up

Starting small means taking it step by step. Don't jump right into advanced training levels without mastering the basics. Start with the basics, focusing on your stance and footwork and getting the fundamentals right. Then, practice the techniques that suit you best, and build on them. You can create a strong foundation for future advanced learning by perfecting the basics.

Have Confidence in Your Skills and Abilities

Wrestling is intimidating, especially when seeing experienced wrestlers in action. But don't let that discourage you. Believing in yourself and your ability to learn and grow like every wrestler is a fundamental attitude. Go into the match with a positive mindset.

Visualize yourself performing, give your best, and focus on the moves you excel in. Believe in your ability and skills, and you will surely ace the game.

Find Mentors Who Can Help You Grow as a Wrestler

Having a mentor makes a substantial difference in your journey as a wrestler. Look out for wrestlers who have been where you are and achieved the goals you set for yourself. Mentors provide you with guidance, motivation, and hands-on training while sharing their experiences. You can learn a lot from the people who have been through what you're going through.

Keep a Positive Attitude and Believe in Yourself

A positive attitude is crucial to success in any field; wrestling is no different. Keeping a positive attitude doesn't mean getting things right all the time. It means having a willingness to learn and improve from mistakes. No wrestler is perfect. However, every mistake can be an opportunity to learn and improve. Keep your spirits high and allow opportunities for yourself to grow and develop your skillsets.

Women can do it. Wrestling has no gender restrictions, and if you set your heart on the game and adopt the tips mentioned above, you can become an ace woman wrestler. Be bold and speak up for yourself, start small and build, have confidence in your skills and abilities, find mentors to guide you, and always keep a positive attitude. Believe in yourself, and you'll achieve your goals in no time. Remember, the more you practice, the better you become, and always be ready to learn more. Then, it's time to hit the mat.

General Pro Wrestling Tips

Whether you're training to become a pro wrestler or a novice, learning the basics and avoiding potential injuries is essential. This section shares some general pro wrestling tips to help you prepare mentally and physically for the challenges ahead.

- **Practice Safely to Avoid Injury:** Wrestling is a contact sport involving many physical contacts, which can result in injuries. Therefore, practicing safe techniques and using protective gear, such as helmets, elbow pads, knee pads, mouthguards, and groin guards, is essential. Always warm up before training or a match to help prevent injuries.

- **Learn the Rules of Professional Wrestling:** You must master the rules of professional wrestling to be a successful wrestler. Studying the different matches, understanding the ring's layout, and learning the specific moves and holds are imperative. Also, watch wrestling matches to learn from other experienced wrestlers.
- **Stay in Shape and Stay Hydrated:** In pro wrestling, endurance, and strength are crucial. Therefore, it's essential to stay in shape by following a balanced diet and an exercise routine that includes cardio and strength training. Also, staying hydrated is vital in any sport for optimal performance. Drink plenty of water before, during, and after training or matches.
- **Listen to Your Body and Respect its Limits:** Knowing your limits is vital in pro wrestling. Pushing yourself too hard can result in injuries, so listening to your body and taking breaks when necessary is crucial. Also, don't take unnecessary risks in matches; always prioritize your safety and that of other wrestlers.
- **Use Visualization to Reach Your Goals:** Visualization is an excellent technique to help you achieve your goals in pro wrestling. For example, imagining yourself executing a perfect move or watching your opponent's moves before the match can help you gain an advantage. Furthermore, visualize how winning feels, which can help increase your confidence and motivation.

A few key things genuinely matter for achieving success in wrestling. Firstly, you must be passionate about the sport. Wrestling is not something you can do half-heartedly and expect to excel. You must be willing to put in the time and effort to train physically and mentally. Moreover, you must have a strong work ethic and an unwavering commitment to your goals.

Whether competing to win a championship or improving your skills, you need an unyielding dedication to your craft. Finally, it would be best to surround yourself with people who will support and encourage you on your journey. Your coaches, teammates, and family members are crucial in helping you succeed on the wrestling mat. You can accomplish anything in wrestling and beyond with passion, hard work, and a robust support system.

Conclusion

Wrestling is one of the oldest and most challenging sports. However, it provides countless benefits and rewards for those willing to put in the time and effort to master its techniques. From posture and balance to advanced maneuvers and techniques, wrestling is a comprehensive sport requiring strength, agility, and a keen mind. So, whether you're a youth, high school, or college athlete or simply looking to get back in shape, wrestling offers an exciting and rewarding challenge to improve your life on and off the mat.

Wrestling involves grappling with an opponent to gain control and pin them to the ground. Several basic rules and techniques every wrestler must master include proper stance, hand placement, and grip. Wrestling aims to get your opponent to the ground and control them using combined moves, such as takedowns, joint locks, and pinning maneuvers. This guide covered the basics of wrestling, from the rules and techniques to advanced moves and strategies. It explored posture and balance fundamentals and how to perform penetrating and lifting maneuvers. It also discussed the art of attacking and countering and how to use reversal techniques effectively.

One of the most critical skills for wrestling success is proper posture and balance. This involves maintaining a low center of gravity, keeping your feet shoulder-width apart, and staying balanced and centered. This skill requires practice and discipline, developed through consistent training and coaching. Wrestling involves several advanced maneuvers and techniques demanding strength, agility, and precision. These maneuvers include penetrating moves, such as double-leg takedowns, single-leg attacks, and lifting and throwing maneuvers requiring quick reflexes and keen timing.

A key aspect of wrestling is to attack and counterattack effectively. This skill involves creating openings and opportunities to score points and anticipate and neutralize your opponent's moves. It necessitates strategic thinking, physical prowess, and mental toughness. This guide provides several exercises and drills to develop your offensive and defensive capabilities.

Wrestling requires a strong understanding of reversal and escape techniques, allowing you to get out of a vulnerable position and regain control of the match. These skills involve quick thinking, agility, and a willingness to take calculated risks to gain an advantage. Finally, wrestling consists of various pinning combinations using physical strength and strategic thinking. These moves allow you to gain control of your opponent and secure a win. But you must learn to adapt to changing circumstances and react quickly to your opponent's moves.

Wrestling is a unique sport that offers mental and physical challenges, making it an ideal choice for those looking to improve their health and fitness. Whether you're interested in competing at a high level or merely want to get back in shape and learn valuable life skills, wrestling is an exciting and rewarding challenge helping you build confidence, discipline, and resilience on and off the mat. So, why not try wrestling and discover how this ancient sport can improve your life?

Good luck on your journey to becoming a skilled wrestler!

Here's another book by Clint Sharp that you might like

References

(N.d.). Wvmat.com. https://www.wvmat.com/overview.htm

History of wrestling & UWW. (n.d.). United World Wrestling. https://uww.org/organisation/history-wrestling-uww

Overview of wrestling rules. (n.d.). Finalsite.net. https://resources.finalsite.net/images/v1583950707/sacredsf/c1vuicxnw1w5xwmwi7vs/wrestling_packet.pdf

Rookie Road. (2019, December 29). What is wrestling? Rookieroad.com; Rookie Road. https://www.rookieroad.com/wrestling/what-is/

The history of wrestling. (2010, June 10). Athleticscholarships.net. https://www.athleticscholarships.net/history-of-wrestling.htm

What Are the Different Types of Wrestling? (2021, February 18). Fitness Quest. https://www.fitnessquest.com/what-are-the-different-types-of-wrestling/

Wikipedia contributors. (2023, May 29). Wrestling. Wikipedia, The Free Encyclopedia. https://en.wikipedia.org/w/index.php?title=Wrestling&oldid=1157634607

Wild Pages Press. (2017a). Wrestling: Notebook. Createspace Independent Publishing Platform.

Wild Pages Press. (2017b). Wrestling: Notebook. Createspace Independent Publishing Platform.

Wrestling facts. (n.d.). Auburntakedown.com. http://www.auburntakedown.com/parents-corner/wrestling-facts.html

www.ingramcontent.com/pod-product-compliance
Lightning Source LLC
Chambersburg PA
CBHW051848160426
43209CB00006B/1206